EAT WELL AND BE HAPPY!

Traditionally Rustic Food: Easy and simple recipes for a healthy, happy, and balanced life

© Carmen Delgado 2021

www.carmensorganickitchen.com

Photography © Shelly Waldman

Photography © Carmen Delgado, pages, 16, 128, 136, 188, 196, 202

Photography Quentin Bacon, pages 10, 183

Carmen's portraits in back cover, Bio and pages 6 & 224 by Nish Photography, Australia

Design, layout and artistic direction: Rosa Mármol

Editing Gowor International Publishing

ISBN: 978-0-6450673-0-9

The moral rights of Carmen Delgado to be identified as the author of this work have been asserted following the Copyright Act

First published in United States of America 2021 by Carmen Delgado

Any opinions expressed in this work are exclusively those of the author and are not necessarily the views held or endorsed by Carmen Delgado.

All rights reserved. No part of this publication may be reproduced or transmitted by any means, electronic, photocopying or otherwise, without prior written permission of the author.

Disclaimer

All the information, techniques, skills, and concepts contained within this publication are of the nature of general comment only and are not in any way recommended as individual advice. The intent is to offer a variety of information to provide a wider range of choices now and in the future, recognising that we all have widely diverse circumstances and viewpoints. Should any reader choose to make use of the information herein, this is their decision, and the author and publisher/s do not assume any responsibilities whatsoever under any conditions or circumstances. The author does not take responsibility for the business, financial, personal or other success, results or fulfilment upon the readers' decision to use this information. It is recommended that the reader obtain independent advice.

Traditionally Rustic Food

EASY & SIMPLE RECIPES FOR A HEALTHY, HAPPY & BALANCED LIFE

Carmen Delgado

To my dear Gabriela, who inspires me to be a better cook.

I love you to the moon and back.

Table of Contents

Foreword 11

Carmen's Story 13

Why Organic? 17

Tips & tricks 19

Staples – Broths, never fail mayonnaise, super-greens pesto, salad dressings
and more 25

Drinks – Seasonal smoothies, hot and cold drinks, and sangria 41

Breakfast – Inspiring ideas for easy and special breakfast 55

Small Bites – Delicious dips and tapas 67

Salads and Vegetable Side Dishes – A rainbow of salads and full of
flavour vegetables 91

Soups - Nourishing, hearty and scrumptious 109

Pasta & Rice – Perfect rice and pasta, easy paella and couscous,
and tasty risotto 127

Fish & Meat – Clams, mussels, salmon, chicken, and beef with
international flavours 151

Bread & Pizza – From easy flatbread to breads of the world and spelt pizza 179

Sweets & Treats – Basic muffins, cakes, cookies, easy ice-cream, sorbet
and chocolate 197

Thank You 221

Index 225

About The Author 229

Carmen's Organic Kitchen
100% Made with Love

Rocky Road
$2 or
3 for $5

100% ORGANIC

Foreword

From the very first moment I was introduced to Carmen, I could feel her love for the art of food preparation.

Cooking isn't just something Carmen does, it's who she is. She pours her heart into the process of creating and preparing dishes that warm the bodies and souls of the people who enjoy them.

Her deep cultural background emerges in every dish she prepares, and her inspiration comes across clearly in the way she teaches her clients and fans to cook.

I am touched and moved by her inspiration for her career and by her desire to share what she knows with those who are ready to take their cooking to a new level.

I know that you will find great joy and nourishment in the pages of her recipe book as you dive into the world of cuisine that she shares with you.

Enjoy the book!

Emily Gowor
INSPIRATIONAL WRITER & SPEAKER

*Carmen at 3 years old at the traditional spring fair in her hometown
(Feria de la Salud, Córdoba, Spain)*

Carmen's Story

I was born in Córdoba, Spain. I am the youngest of six siblings. My memory of family and food comes from my early years. I remember when the milkman came to our street, the small greengrocer in the corner, where all seasonal fruits and vegetables looked and tasted beautiful, our local butcher, and the small fish shop. I loved going grocery shopping with my mother. The food was simple but very important.

I have always been interested in food and I started cooking from an early age, although I wasn't very successful at the start.

In my early adulthood, I decided to follow my dream to learn to speak English and to further my University studies. I then embarked on my first USA adventure.

Two years later, I ended up going to Australia, where I graduated with an MBA and met my husband. Yes, LOVE... isn't it what moves the world? We met on a blind date, believing that we were from the same town. And we are, but from different countries, on different continents; my husband was born in Córdoba, Argentina. Some will call it coincidence, but I strongly believe it was destiny. We married in Melbourne, Australia on the day of my parent's 50th wedding anniversary. Our happiness was completed when our daughter Gabriela was born.

As I mentioned earlier, my interest in food started in my childhood, but it was after I married that I started being more involved and began experimenting. I successfully helped my husband on his journey to be fitter and healthier through good nutritious food. When my daughter started eating solids, I turned to my roots and cooked all her meals from scratch, as I had seen my sisters do with their children.

After a health fright, I was advised to take on a hobby that complimented my logical accounting work and mind. I tried many things: knitting (I love it, but it wasn't enough at the time), dancing (I always wanted to be a dancer)... but nothing seemed to work. It was a dear friend who pointed out that I should start cooking more, as I was very good at it and passionate about my food. Bless him!

Carmen's Organic Kitchen was created in 2014. I sold my own range of organic products in markets. I volunteered as a head cook at my daughter's school canteen. I also volunteered at our local primary school with their kitchen program. These were very happy times. It was clear that the kitchen is my happy place.

When my new USA adventure took me to California, I was determined to pursue my cooking and food career. I started teaching cooking, mainly to children, which I love. However, being a world citizen, I needed to be able to take my work wherever I may go next. That's when the idea of writing this book came to my mind.

I feel compelled to share my success in the kitchen, following a simple, balanced, and healthy diet. I believe 'you are what you eat'. So, if you eat well, you will live well and be happy.

As Ferrán Adriá said in Spanish television, I am telling my story through my food, my recipes nourish the soul and feed the body.

Traditionally Rustic Food is my way of helping you get back to basics in the kitchen.

In this day and age where there are so many different diets to follow, it can get very confusing and overwhelming when it comes to choosing what to feed your loved ones. In this book, I have collected some of my basic recipes that are quick and easy to cook and enjoyable to eat. I have developed these recipes during my years living overseas, using local and organic produce.

Believe it or not, produce tastes different from one place to the other. The soil, the weather, and the sun exposure all affect how an ingredient tastes and grows. A recipe that you have cooked many times, will taste very different when you cook it in another place. Imagine the difference when you cook it in a different country, and more so in the opposite hemisphere!

Well, I've had the opportunity to do all the testing for you. All you have to do is:

- get your apron on
- follow my clear steps
- add love
- make the recipe your own
- and have fun!

The idea is for you to make a weekly menu including all food groups to achieve a balanced diet: white meat, fish, rice, pulses (legumes), red meat, pasta, and something more special for the weekend. Include a side dish or salad, some bread, rice or basic couscous, and you will have a complete a delicious meal each day! If you are *VEGETARIAN* or follow a *PLANT-BASED*, *GLUTEN-FREE* and/or *DAIRY-FREE* diet, check the notes and options at the end of the recipes. This book is all-inclusive.

Balance is very important in all aspects of our lives. Having a balanced life will ensure happiness. Isn't that what we all pursue? Look through this book and start selecting the recipes that call to you first. Always follow your instinct. Create your weekly menu, write your grocery shopping list, head to the shops (stores), and start your new culinary journey with me.

Some of the recipes are connected to someone special in my life. People that I have met along the way. You will get to know them and how they are connected to the recipe and to me.

Traditionally Rustic Food is a reference cookbook for anybody with any level of cooking skills. It is written as if I was in my cooking classes, using clear instructions and plain language. It is enjoyable to read and an interactive cookbook at the same time.

This book will help you to:

- Easy meal planning
- Learn and increase your cooking skills
- Easy grocery shopping experience
- Less time in the kitchen
- Making cooking enjoyable
- Healthy eating
- Bonding time with family
- Mental and physical wellbeing

Quoting P.T. Barnum: *"The noblest art is that of making others happy".*

My aim with this book is to bring happiness into your kitchen and your life, and for you to make others happy through the food that you will cook.

EAT WELL AND BE HAPPY!

Why Organic?

"Never underestimate the way a good meal could change the world."

DEWEY DENOUEMENT (A Series of Unfortunate Events)

When I heard this quote watching TV with my daughter, I ran to get my notebook and wrote it down. What a powerful message this is! We can certainly change the world by using the right food and adopting a sustainable way of living.

What we call *ORGANIC* today is the way our ancestors grew and ate food in the past. Think of the people in small rural areas in Italy, Greece, or Spain who are still living off the land. These people live a healthier lifestyle, because they receive all the vitamins and nutrients their bodies need from the food they eat.

I'm not suggesting here that we all have our own veggie patch. I certainly don't have a green thumb and I haven't even been successful at growing my own herbs. There are other ways you can source organic food. Farmers and local markets are a great place to begin. They are fun for the whole family and you will also be able to speak with the growers directly to know about their organic farming principles.

There are also online providers that work directly with farmers. These are a great and very convenient option. I use them all the time. Some of them offer a set box of seasonal fruit and vegetables. I like to call it 'the mystery box'. I love this option as it allows me to get creative in the kitchen.

Your local greengrocer and independent supermarkets are also good places to buy your food. I use these to find the 'missing ingredients'. I still support my local community without breaking the budget; look for weekly specials.

Then you have the larger food suppliers offering local and organic produce. These are great for bulk food shopping. You can get better quality ingredients at a cheaper price and avoid packaging. Some of them allow you to bring your own containers, making your storing easier.

When it comes to meat and fish, my preference is to shop at small and local stores wherever possible. Also, your local and farmers markets are a good choice. Butchers know which farm the animal was raised in and what part of the animal a particular cut came from. They usually have long term relationships with the farmers. In the same way, fishmongers also have good relationships with local fishermen and they tend to take pride in selecting local and sustainably fished options. It may seem more expensive, but the quality and the flavour are well worth it.

The larger food grocers usually have a butcher and fish department with clear information on where the produce comes from as well as its grade of sustainability. Look at their weekly specials and design your weekly menu using those cheaper products. This approach will help you keep a reasonable budget without compromising quality in the food you provide to your loved ones. When one of my favourite cuts of meat or fish is on special, I usually buy more than I need and freeze them. I find it very useful to have food that I can always reach for when I haven't got time to get to the shops.

Remember, you are what you eat, so pay careful attention to what you ingest. I'm not a big fan of packaged food. If I buy these products, then I carefully read the list of ingredients. If I see something that I don't recognise, I put it back on the shelf.

As Michael Pollan says: *"Don't eat anything your great-grandmother wouldn't recognize as food."*

My gift for you is to have fun from the moment you start thinking about what you are going to cook to the time you actually cook it, always with a sustainable mindset. Our planet and our bodies are precious and we need to take good care of them. After all, we only have one body and there is only one Earth.

Tips & Tricks

🔲 BAKING

The best oven temperature when baking cakes and cupcakes is 160C (320F). Even when the recipe requests a higher temperature, I trust my instinct as it is better to have a lower oven temperature. I find that cakes, cupcakes and sponges tend to cook more evenly and I avoid the risk of them sinking. This usually happens when the oven is too hot. Believe me, I've been there and it's not fun to see your hard work destroyed.

Always preheat the oven after you have your batter ready to bake. You will get better results by giving your batter time to rest before being baked. In addition, set the timer 5 minutes before the suggested baking time (unless otherwise indicated in the recipe), it is better to add extra minutes than to have overbaked goodies.

BAKING FLOUR

Baking flour is the best to make light cakes and sponges. Although you can buy this special flour, it is easier to make as you need it and it is much cheaper too.

All you need is plain (all-purpose) flour and cornflour (cornstarch). The rule of thumb is: for every cup of flour (150gr, approximately) you remove 2 Tablespoons (20gr, approximately) and substitute with 2 Tablespoons cornstarch (cornflour). Do the numbers and calculate depending on how much flour the recipe requires and mix them well.

It is said that for best results you should sift baking flour up to 6 times, but I usually just sift it on the spot, and it always works. When I have time and when I am making a special cake, I always take the time to sift the flour all the way, to make the lightest cake.

BUTTERMILK

Buttermilk is the easiest thing to make on the spot. Add 2 teaspoons of vinegar or lemon juice to a cup of full cream (whole) milk (250ml / 8 oz). Let it set for a few minutes and you have freshly made buttermilk ready to use in any recipe. For best results, the milk should be at room temperature. I like using organic unfiltered apple cider vinegar for its health benefits.

EGGS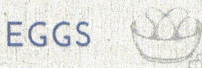

When cooking with eggs, it is best if they are at room temperature. Buy the best farm fresh organic eggs that you can find, they may be a bit more expensive, but well worth it. You may even get a double yolk!

GLUTEN-FREE FLOUR

My favourite *GLUTEN-FREE* flour for baking cakes and muffins is *Bob's Red Mill* 1:1 *GLUTEN-FREE Baking Flour*. You can use this flour in place of any wheat flour in the *SWEETS & TREATS* recipes in this book.

HERBS

When using herbs, the best ratio for flavour is 1 teaspoon of dry, or 1 Tablespoon of fresh herbs.

Try to have some fresh herbs, but always keep a good pantry of your favourite dry herbs.

I like using fresh herbs to finish a dish and in salads, but when making stews and soups I prefer to use dry as I find that they release more flavour.

For all stock (broth) recipes in this book, you can substitute the dry herbs for a *bouquet garni*[1]. You can find this in tea bags or loose leaves. Use 1 teabag per recipe or 1 teaspoon if loose.

OIL

I only cook with *EXTRA VIRGIN OLIVE OIL (EVOO)*. I use it for any type of cuisine, including Asian and Indian. I do not find its flavour overpowers that of the sauces and spices.

When baking, I prefer to heat the *extra virgin olive oil* with a slice of lemon peel until is lightly brown. I then let it cool down before using it. If you're short of time, just add the oil straight from the bottle or buy *Light Olive Oil*. I use this type of oil for deep frying.

---

[1] The bouquet garni is a bundle of herbs usually tied together with string and mainly used to prepare soup, stock, casseroles and various stews. (en.wikipedia.or)

 ONIONS

Brown onion is a staple in my kitchen. I like this type of onion for any cooking.

I use *red* (purple, or as they called them in Australia, '*Spanish*') onion when I cook with tomato. Being a sweeter onion, I find that I don't need to add sugar when I make meals that contain tomatoes. I also use red onion for all my raw recipes, although I like to macerate it in lemon juice while I prepare the rest of the ingredients.

I learned that trick from my long time friend Ana Mérida. I find this takes the heat from the flavour of the raw onion, and makes it more pleasant to eat.

 MEASUREMENTS

I use metric units in my recipes: 250ml cup, 20ml (4 teaspoons) Tablespoon, and 5ml teaspoon. If you use 15ml (3 teaspoons) Tablespoon, for most recipes the difference won't matter, unless you're measuring baking powder or cornflour (cornstarch). For these, add an extra teaspoon for every Tablespoon required.

If you use US measuring cups, make sure you use them for the whole recipe; you will get the same results.

I have calculated all weight conversions using a precise scale, as well as converting into measuring cups.

POTATOES

My preferred potatoes are *Desiree* or *red potatoes*, always organic and locally grown, when possible. These potatoes have more fibre than other types and are useful for all methods of cooking.

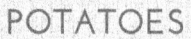 RECIPES

I always recommend my students to read any recipe at least twice, making sure they understand all directions and steps, the cooking process, cooking times, serving size, and that they can perform the required techniques.

My recipes are easy to follow and read (at least that's my intention when I write them), but I still encourage you to read them a couple of times to understand all parts of the recipe, before you even think on start getting any ingredients ready.

I have written suggestions and tips, usually at the end of the recipes that can be beneficial before you start cooking.

 PEPPER

I love the flavour of freshly ground black pepper. This is the only pepper I use in my kitchen; that's why it is the only one in my recipes. However, you can use any pepper that you like. My advice here is to buy really good peppercorns and grind them, as you need them. This ensures more freshness and better flavour.

SALAD IN A JAR

Any salad recipe from this book can be put into a jar. This is a great way to take food to work, or even on a picnic. Get yourself a few 3 cups capacity mason jars, for individual lunches. Prepare the ingredients as per the recipe of your choice and fill the jar in the following order:

1. Dressing
2. Protein (if any)
3. Beans and/or pulses
4. Nuts, seeds, and olives
5. Hard vegetables (beetroot, carrots, potatoes)
6. Soft vegetables (cucumber, green beans, tomato)
7. Lettuce or salad leaves

The idea is that the dressing does not wilt the softest leaves and vegetables and infuses the protein. When you are ready to eat your salad, or serve it at a picnic, turn the jar upside down over a bowl. The dressing will cover the whole salad and all ingredients will be nice and crispy. There's no excuse to buy lunch anymore!

SELF-RAISING FLOUR

This is a staple in Australia, but not so easy to find in the USA. Self-raising flour is super easy to make. In fact, I haven't bought it for a long time. I always make my own as I need it. For every cup (150gr) of flour, you add 2 teaspoons of baking powder and mix well until fully combined. Next time you come across a recipe that requires self-raising flour, you know what to do.

SERVING (OR PORTION) SIZE

My recipes are based on a single portion size of 250gr (0.55 lb) of both protein and vegetables. For salads, I have calculated them as a side dish and also as a shared meal at the table. If you are going to make them your main lunch or supper meal, all salad recipes are perfect for 2 good dishes or 3 smaller servings.

SUGAR

I use raw sugar for most baking, except when I bake with chocolate. For this, I like using panela or coconut sugar. These sugars are less processed than normal white sugar. They also give a light caramel and warm taste. But they're still sugar, so don't abuse them!

UTENSILS

The main utensil in my organic kitchen is a large wooden spoon. It works with all pots and pans and it is made of natural material. I have measuring cups and spoons and a couple of measuring glass jugs (pitchers).

For pots and pans, I have my beloved pressure cooker and a couple of heavy bottom pots (one medium and one large) for soups and boiling pasta or vegetables. I mainly cook with a *Lodge* cast iron pan, unless I'm cooking Asian or Indian Food, then I use my *Green Pan* wok. I have a special *EVACO* non-stick ceramic fry pan for cooking eggs only. It's very important to have a dedicated pan to make the *SPANISH TORTILLA* (Page 78). I have a couple of smaller saucepans and a deep casserole for deep-frying.

For baking, I have a large sheet pan (baking tray) that's perfect for 1 sheet pan dinners. I also have a couple of smaller baking trays. For cakes, I have square and round cake tins, a bundt or flute cake pan, and two different sized muffins baking trays.

I like using a Chinese cleaver for chopping, but this is not comfortable for everyone. My advice is that you get a proper and good quality chef's knife. Its size will be determined by your height. Go to a knife or kitchen shop (store) and let the professionals help you choose the best knife for you. Trust me, this will make your cooking time more enjoyable. You also need a pairing knife for small jobs and a serrated knife for cutting tomatoes.

I always go to second hand shops when I need a new gadget in the kitchen. Most of the time I find great bargains. Remember that one person's trash is another person's treasure. This is a great way to be sustainable in your kitchen.

Staples

"Cooking is like love. It should be entered into with abandon or not at all."

HARRIET VAN HOME

VEGETABLE STOCK (BROTH)

Making stock (broth) is a great way to start your culinary journey. This broth is the base of many of the recipes in this book. It is so good, that you will be happy to have it on its own as a cup of comforting consommé. Homemade stocks are an essential staple in my kitchen. I hope they are in yours very soon. They are the reason I considered to start my cooking career. Whenever I got complimented for the flavour in my food, I thought of the ingredients I had used and there always was one of my broths. One day, I was told I should bottle them and sell them, and that's when I started thinking about sharing my food with you!

1. Prepare a large and deep pot
2. Wash all vegetables thoroughly and chopped them roughly
3. Place chopped vegetables, garlic, dry (or fresh) herbs, bay leave, peppercorns and salt in the pot
4. Add water and bring to the boil
5. Simmer broth for 1 to 1.5 hours
6. Take off the heat and let set for 15 minutes
7. Drain stock over a double strainer or a fine sieve (use a flour sack towel, muslin or cheesecloth)
8. Keep fresh broth in the fridge for up to 2 days
9. Freeze it in small recycled jars for 3 to 4 months (don't forget to label them!)

Use this stock (broth) for your favourite vegetarian and *PLANT-BASED* soups, add it to stews, curries, or any recipe that requires liquid. The more flavour you add, the better your dish will taste.

You can double the recipe and increase the simmering time to 2 hours.

This recipe works well using a *PRESSURE COOKER* or *INSTANT POT*. In both cases, cook on a high option for ½ hour; let rest for 5 minutes and quickly release the steam. Wait 5 extra minutes before opening the lid. I find the flavour is more intense while taking a shorter time to cook.

INGREDIENTS

MAKES 6 CUPS
(1.5 LITRES / 48 OZ)

- 8 cups water (2 litres / 64 oz / or to cover the vegetables)
- 2 medium carrots
- 200gr (7 oz) celery stalks with leaves
- 1 leek
- 1 fennel bulb
- 1 medium brown onion
- 1 large garlic clove, smashed and peeled
- ½ teaspoon dry parsley (or 2 teaspoons fresh)
- ½ teaspoon dry thyme (or 2 teaspoons fresh)
- ¼ teaspoon dry rosemary (or 1 teaspoon fresh)
- 1 dry bay leave
- 12 whole black peppercorns
- 1 Tablespoon salt

Staples

CHICKEN STOCK (BROTH)

INGREDIENTS

MAKES 6 CUPS
(1.5 LITRES / 48 OZ)

- 8 cups water (2 litres / 64 oz)
- 1 raw chicken carcass or 1kg (2.2 lb) raw chicken bones
- 1 medium carrot
- 2 celery stalks with leaves
- 1 medium brown onion
- 2 large garlic cloves, smashed and peeled
- ½ teaspoon dry parsley (or 2 teaspoons fresh)
- ½ teaspoon dry thyme (or 2 teaspoons fresh)
- ¼ teaspoon dry rosemary (or 1 teaspoon fresh)
- 1 dry bay leave
- 12 whole black peppercorns
- 1 Tablespoon salt

Chicken stock (broth) is my favourite. You can use it in any recipe that uses stock, even if cooking another type of meat. Let's face it! We're not restaurants that need all types of meat broths. At our home kitchen we want flavour but also to simplify our cooking time. I admire you if you make all types of stock, but this chicken broth is enough for anything you want to cook and will give you great results. I always use the carcass from a chicken that my husband debones for the BBQ. If I don't have time to make the stock, I freeze the carcass, so I have it ready to use any time. I even make the broth with the carcass still frozen. Ask your butcher for chicken bones, many of them give them out for free. If you can't find a chicken carcass, use chicken necks. These are usually quite cheap and make a great stock.

1. Place chicken bones in a large and deep pot
2. Pour water and bring to the boil
3. Skim all impurities and foam that comes to the surface
4. Wash carrots and celery thoroughly and cut into chunks
5. Cut onion in quarters
6. Place carrots, celery, onion, garlic, dry (or fresh) herbs, bay leave peppercorns and salt in the pot
7. Simmer broth for 2 to 2.5 hours
8. Take off the heat and let set for 15 minutes
9. Drain stock over a double strainer or a fine sieve (use a flour sack towel, muslin or cheesecloth)
10. Keep fresh broth in the fridge for up to 2 days
11. Freeze it in small recycled jars for 2 to 3 months (don't forget to label them!)

This stock (broth) will warm your soul. The smell in my kitchen, when it's simmering, makes me happy.

You can also double this recipe and increase simmering time to 3 to 3.5 hours. This recipe works well using a *PRESSURE COOKER* or *INSTANT POT*. Cook in a high position for 45 minutes; let rest for 5 minutes and quickly release the steam. Wait 5 extra minutes before opening the lid.

FISH STOCK (BROTH)

Fish stock is another useful staple to have in your kitchen. Whenever you buy fish, be sure to ask for the bones. You can freeze these for later use or just make the broth fresh on the spot and freeze it. You can also use fish heads, but with these, you need to skim the stock as they leave more impurities. It is also better if you double strain the broth, using clean utensils each time. White fish makes the best and clearer stock. Fish broth is a great alternative to have a quick noodle soup if you don't eat chicken, or simply prefer fish.

1. Prepare a large and deep pot
2. Wash fish bones and vegetables and chopped them roughly
3. Place fish bones, vegetables, garlic, and parsley into the pot
4. Drizzle with olive oil and mix until well combined
5. Add lemon juice, peppercorns, and salt
6. Pour water and bring to the boil
7. Simmer broth for 20 to 25 minutes
8. Take off the heat and let set for 5 minutes
9. Drain stock over a double strainer or a fine sieve (use a flour sack towel, muslin, or cheesecloth)
10. Keep fresh broth in the fridge for up to 2 days
11. Freeze it in small recycled jars for 1 to 2 months (don't forget to label them!)

INGREDIENTS
MAKES 6 CUPS
(1.5 LITRES / 48 OZ)

- 8 cups water (2 litres / 64 oz)
- 1 kg (2.2 lb) fish bones
- 1 bunch green/spring onions (scallions)
- 2 large garlic cloves, smashed and peeled
- Juice of ½ lemon (o more if needed)
- 1 handful of fresh parsley, stalks included
- 1 Tablespoon olive oil
- 12 whole black peppercorns
- 1 teaspoon salt

Staples

SEAFOOD FUMET

Fumet is a French culinary term that means stock or broth. In my organic kitchen fumet means seafood stock. This is the one I make for my *SEAFOOD PAELLA* (Page 139). I learned this term from my sister Mayte and her husband Jeronimo. They live in the Levante area in Spain, where *Paella Valenciana* was born. I always thought that *Fumet* was a word from Valencia which refers to seafood broth, and that is why I call it this way. I use prawn (shrimp) heads and shells to make this stock. You can also add some fish bones for extra flavour, but I like the seafood flavour by itself. This is a very simple, but very smelly, broth to make. My husband always sends me to make it outside. Keep your windows open or cook it out of the house, if possible. It is also very cheap, as you use something that you will otherwise throw away. I am sure once you try it the first time, you will keep making it all the time you need it.

1. Heat olive oil in a large and deep pot over medium heat
2. Sauté the prawn (shrimp) heads and shells until they change in colour, for about 5 minutes
3. Add onion, garlic, bay leaf, and peppercorns
4. Pour water and bring to the boil
5. Add salt, reduce heat and simmer for 30 minutes
6. Take off the heat and let set for 5 minutes
7. Drain stock over a double strainer or a fine sieve (use a flour sack towel, muslin, or cheesecloth)
8. Keep fresh broth in the fridge for up to 2 days
9. Freeze it in small recycled jars for 1 to 2 months (don't forget to label them!)

Use this stock to make any seafood dish, you will take it to another level of cooking. For a simple seafood soup, add some fresh fish and seafood to the broth with your favourite noodles or pasta. Your loved ones will be delighted! And so will you.

INGREDIENTS
MAKES 6 CUPS
(1.5 LITRES / 48 OZ)

- 8 cups water (2 litres / 64 oz)
- ½ kg (1.1 lb) prawn (shrimp) heads and shells (from 8 large whole prawns/shrimps)
- 1 medium brown onion, roughly chopped
- 1 large garlic clove, smashed and peeled
- 1 Tablespoon olive oil
- 1 dry bay leaf
- 6 whole black peppercorns
- 1 teaspoon salt

GARLIC & PARSLEY BLEND

INGREDIENTS
MAKES 1 ½ CUPS

- 1 whole bunch fresh flat parsley
- 2 whole garlic heads, peeled

This aromatic blend is a very important staple in Spanish cooking. I was lucky to collaborate and work with my friend Noemi in her Spanish catering business in Melbourne when she reintroduced this versatile spice to me. We became friends instantly. Our passion for food and everything Spanish brought us together. She has babysat my daughter, helped me when I was sick, driven me to the airport on my first solo trip to Spain; the list goes on and on. When I was asked to cater lunch for the year 12th graduation at our school, I reached to her for advice, and there she was, cooking next to me on the day. These memories will live with me forever. Whenever I make or use the blend, I always think of her.

1. In a food processor, place parsley and garlic
2. Blend in pulses until you achieve a finely chopped consistency
3. Place blend in a jar and keep in the fridge for up to 2 months

Many of my recipes in this book request this blend, but you will start using it in many more.

It works very well with grilled fish, to give extra flavour to your breaded food or to add to stews and soups.

Once you start using it, you will not be able to cook without it anymore.

Staples

NEVER FAIL MAYONNAISE

Homemade mayonnaise is very easy to make and very rewarding. Follow the steps below and you will have creamy and delicious mayonnaise anytime. All you need is a good hand (stick) blender, good ingredients, and a steady hand. My sister Rosa taught me how to make it. I love her so much! We are the two youngest siblings and we grew up being very close. The stories I could tell you about our childhood…

The mayonnaise that we know today was created by a French Chef to celebrate the victory of Mahon, in the Balearic Islands in Spain, in the 18th century. That is where its name comes from and also its popularity in Spanish food.

1. In a deep bowl or jar place the whole egg, lemon juice, ¼ cup oil, salt and pepper
2. Place the hand (stick) blender to the bottom of the bowl or jar
3. Start the blender on low speed WITHOUT MOVING THE STICK
4. When you see that all ingredients are combined and it starts looking like mayonnaise, SLOWLY pour the oil, ¼ cup at a time, and start moving the blender until the mixture thickens
5. Check for seasoning and spoon into a jar or storage container
6. Mayonnaise can be kept in the fridge for up to 5 days

As a good Spaniard, I like the strong and bitter flavour of extra virgin olive oil. If you prefer a milder mayonnaise, use avocado or sunflower seed oil. You can also mix the extra virgin olive oil with another lighter oil, or use a light olive oil.

Mayonnaise is the base for *Alioli*, Pink, or Cocktail Sauce (*Salsa Rosa*) and *Tartar Sauce*.

To make *Alioli* (Aioli), pound 1 small garlic with the salt in a mortar and pestle and add the resulting paste in step 1 of the recipe above.

To make *Salsa Rosa*, mix 1 Tablespoon of ketchup (tomato sauce), 1 Tablespoon of whiskey, and ¼ teaspoon cayenne pepper or *Tabasco* to your homemade mayonnaise.

To make a simple *Tartar Sauce*, add ¼ cup finely chopped pickled cucumbers or gherkins and 1 teaspoon dry parsley or dill (whichever you prefer or have in your pantry) to your finished mayonnaise.

INGREDIENTS
MAKES 1 CUP

- 1 egg
- ¾ cup (180ml / 6 oz) extra virgin olive oil
- Juice of ½ lemon
- ½ teaspoon salt
- Freshly ground black pepper

IN ADDITION

Always check for seasoning after you have mixed all ingredients. In some cases, you may like to add extra lemon juice.

You can also make spicy mayonnaise adding any spices of your choice. Experiment and enjoy it!

BASIC QUINOA

INGREDIENTS

MAKES 4 TO 6 SERVINGS
(AS A SIDE DISH)

- 1 cup dry quinoa
- 1 cup (250ml / 8 oz) VEGETABLE STOCK (BROTH; Page 27)

From the *Quechua 'kinwa or kinuwa'*, quinoa was a sacred crop to the Incas. It almost disappeared with the arrival of the Spanish (sorry!). But fortunately, it was reintroduced in the 70's and now we can all enjoy this ancient grain. In fact, quinoa is grown as a grain, but it is actually a seed. It's related to spinach and its leaves can be eaten as a super green. Quinoa is *GLUTEN-FREE* and a rich source of manganese and phosphorus. My first contact with quinoa was through the organic cereal that I used to give my baby daughter for breakfast. It had quinoa in it and she loved it! I started investigating and came to know about its bitter after taste and the best way to cook it. This recipe is what I call 15 x 3 basic quinoa. I hope you find it useful and eat lots of it!

1. Soak dry quinoa in cold water for 15 minutes
2. Strain it and rinse well under running water, this removes its bitter aftertaste
3. Place quinoa in a cooking pot and add 1 cup of broth/stock (to add more flavour), bring a the boil, cover, and simmer for 15 minutes
4. Once quinoa is cooked, **DO NOT OPEN THE LID** and let rest for 15 minutes
5. Uncover and separate the grains with a fork
6. Perfectly cooked quinoa is now ready to be served or use in salads

I like to serve it as a side dish with stews and saucy meals. Use it instead of couscous for a *GLUTEN-FREE* option.

Check the quinoa and roasted vegetables salad recipe on my blog. Use the QR code at the end of this book.

PASSATA - BASIC ITALIAN TOMATO SAUCE

Italians have a great tradition for making their own tomato sauce, what in the US is called *marinara sauce*. I was lucky to be invited to one passata making day with my friend Angela's mum. I will never forget the experience. We cooked 3 boxes of Roma (grape) tomatoes in really big pots. We passed the cooked tomatoes through a machine that crushed and strained them. We got a beautiful sauce ready to be used. We then bottled some 48 750ml (24 oz) jars and canned them to be stored until ready to be used. I went home with 12 jars of tomato sauce and a beautiful family and cooking experience. This recipe is my quick version for you to make at home any time, without compromising the quality or the flavour.

1. Place a pan over medium heat, wait about 1 minute for it to get hot, and then add the olive oil
2. In the meantime, chop the onion and garlic and sauté for 3 to 5 minutes over medium heat, until onion is translucent
3. Pour wine or broth and let reduce, for about 1 to 2 minutes
4. Add tomato puree and stir
5. Add dry herbs, one at a time, and stir until well combined
6. Now is the time to add the maple syrup or honey (if using). This will help with the acidity of the tomatoes. However, the red onion is sweet, and I suggest that you taste it and decide if it needs the extra sweetness
7. Simmer for 15 minutes
8. Season with salt and pepper to taste

To use as pizza sauce, let it cool before spreading.

For pasta sauce, place a small ladle of sauce over cooked pasta on each plate, or mix it with the cooked pasta in a pot and serve.

I doubt you will buy store bought pasta or pizza sauce again.

INGREDIENTS
MAKES 1 ½ CUPS

- 1 tin (can) tomato puree (400gr / 14.5 oz)
- 1 small red onion (or ½ medium)
- 1 clove garlic
- 1 Tablespoon olive oil
- ½ teaspoon dry oregano
- ½ teaspoon dry thyme
- ¼ teaspoon dry rosemary
- 1 Tablespoon white wine
- 1 Tablespoon red wine (wine can be substituted for vegetable stock / broth)
- Salt & pepper to taste
- 1 teaspoon maple syrup or honey (optional)

SALAD DRESSING

I love making my own salad dressing. It's easy and its flavour can't be compared with any of the store bought products. I usually make enough to dress one salad, but sometimes I make double and keep it in a jar. My husband and I eat lots of salads, so having some ready-made dressing, makes my meal preparations quicker. I learned from my friend, Rinaldo, not to dress salads and let everybody dress their own. This is a great tip, as you can eat any leftover salad as good as freshly made. Besides, this allows dressing the salad to your own liking. I usually place the dressing at the table in a small bowl with a serving spoon, or in a squeeze bottle.

1. Mix all ingredients in a jar or bowl
2. Taste by dipping 1 salad leave
3. Adjust seasoning and serve

Lemon dressing is my basic salad dressing recipe. It's my favourite and the one that goes with most salads.

Aceto Balsamico is a bit sweeter than pure balsamic vinegar.

I prefer the subtle flavour of Dijon mustard, but you can use any other mustard of your choice.

INGREDIENTS

LEMON DRESSING

- 1 Tablespoon lemon juice (approximately ½ lemon)
- ¼ cup (60ml / 2 oz) extra virgin olive oil
- ¼ teaspoon salt
- Freshly ground black pepper to taste

ACETO DRESSING

- 1 lemon dressing recipe
- ¼ teaspoon Aceto Balsamico de Modena

MUSTARD DRESSING

- 1 lemon dressing recipe
- ¼ teaspoon Dijon Mustard

SUPER GREENS & WALNUTS PESTO

INGREDIENTS
MAKES 1 CUP

- 1 cup basil leaves
- 1 cup super green leaves (spinach, kale, chard, or a mix of them)
- 100gr (0.22 lb / 3.5 oz) walnuts
- 1 large garlic, or 2 small
- ½ cup oil (125ml / 4 oz), plus extra if needed
- 50gr (0.11 lb) parmesan cheese
- ½ teaspoon salt
- 6 black peppercorns

I started making this pesto in California. My love for using local produce made me start making pesto with Californian walnuts. As a mother, I always hide as many vegetables as I can when cooking for my daughter; that's where the idea of the super greens came from. This pesto is very tasty and very healthy at the same time. You can use it as a spread for sandwiches or wraps. It will take them to another level of flavour, trust me.

1. If the walnuts are raw, roast them in a pan over medium heat until you can smell the oils, shaking the pan constantly. Once roasted, place them on a plate to cool down and set aside
2. In a mortar and pestle add salt, peppercorns, and garlic and pound until it forms a smooth paste
3. Place parmesan cheese and walnuts into a food processor and process until just grated
4. Add basil leaves, super greens, oil, and garlic paste to the cheese and walnuts and continue processing until smooth and well combined
5. Place pesto in a jar and cover with a layer of olive oil to preserve it
6. Close the jar and keep refrigerated for up to 1 week

Pesto can be frozen in small cubes for future dressings or easy add on flavour to soups and stews.

Serve it with *GNOCCHI* (Page 136) or *SPELT PASTA* (Page 128).

Drinks

"It's a fairly recent thing but I've become very fond of making drinks myself."

UTADA HIKARU

GREEN SMOOTHIE

INGREDIENTS
MAKES 3 CUPS

WINTER

- 1 medium carrot
- 1 celery stick
- 1 whole orange
- 2 good handfuls green leaves of your choice (spinach, kale, chard, mixed greens)
- 1 apple
- 2cm (1") piece fresh ginger
- 2cm (1") piece fresh turmeric root (or ½ teaspoon ground turmeric)
- 1 cup (250ml / 8 oz) of water

Pureed fruit drinks have existed in Mediterranean and Eastern cultures for hundreds of years. Also, in South and Latin America fruit-based drinks have been staples in their daily diets.[2] Other than fruit juices, I became familiar with green smoothies during my school canteen cooking years. The lovely Kemi Nekvapil, one of the volunteers and active school mum (a great Author, Speaker, and Coach) introduced a green smoothie to the canteen menu. This recipe is based on the one she used to make, with my twist to use seasonal fruit.

WINTER GREEN SMOOTHIE

I base this recipe on the phrase "*an apple a day keeps the doctor away*", the plentiful of delicious apples in autumn (fall) and winter, and the cold healing benefits from ginger. The addition of turmeric is for its anti-inflammatory and other health benefits.[3]

1. Wash carrot and celery thoroughly and cut them into chunks
2. Peel the orange with a potato peeler, being careful to keep the white skin
3. Wash green leaves
4. Cut the apple in quarters and core
5. Peel ginger and turmeric
6. Place all ingredients into a powerful blender or food processor
7. Add water and blend until you get the desired consistency
8. Add extra water for a thinner and lighter drink

I love having this smoothie after my workouts. I feel it nourishes my body (and soul) and hydrates me at the same time.

---

[2] https://behealthy.today

[3] https://draxe.com/nutrition/herbs/turmeric-curcumin-benefits/

— *Drinks* —

GREEN SMOOTHIE

SUMMER GREEN SMOOTHIE

This recipe is very similar to the winter one. I like using tropical and stone summer fruits and berries. I have taken the ginger off but still like keeping the turmeric.

1. Wash carrot and celery thoroughly and cut them into chunks
2. Peel the orange with a potato peeler, being careful to keep the white skin
3. Wash spinach leaves and basil (if using)
4. Peel and cut the mango
5. Peel the turmeric
6. Place all ingredients into a powerful blender or food processor
7. Add water and blend until you get the desired consistency
8. Add extra water for a thinner and lighter drink

If oranges are not available, you can substitute the water for orange juice.

I love to include mango in this smoothie, but I use any stone fruit or berries (or a mix) before they go to waste. This is a great way to use all those not too good-looking fruits and veggies.

A meal in a glass on the hot summer days!

INGREDIENTS
MAKES 3 CUPS

SUMMER

- 1 mango (or 1 cup of any stone summer fruit or fresh berries)
- 1 orange
- 1 medium carrot
- 1 celery stick
- 2 good handfuls spinach leaves (add some fresh basil too)
- 2cm (1") piece fresh turmeric root (or ½ teaspoon ground turmeric)
- 1 cup (250ml / 8 oz) of water

AGUA FRESCA

Agua fresca or *'fresh waters'* has a long tradition in Mexico and Central America. I came to know about it living in California. Now it's one of my favourite drinks in summer and for parties. Its origin goes back to the 15th century when Aztecs farmers would paddle their canoes looking for a ripe fruit to mash and mix with water for a refreshing drink.

Although traditionally sweetened with sugar or agave syrup, I like using honey. During my first trip to Spain after moving to the US, I made agua fresca for my daughter and her friends. Our Spanish neighbour Cheli produces her own honey and she gave me a jar to try and use in the agua fresca. Ever since, I always use honey when making this refreshing drink.

1. Place fruit, honey, and 1 cup of water in a powerful blender or food processor
2. Blend until well combined
3. Add remaining water and stir

To serve, put agua fresca in a jar (pitcher) and add some ice.

When using berries, strain the agua fresca before serving, to remove the seeds.

INGREDIENTS
MAKES 4 TO 6 DRINKS

- 1 cup ripe fruit of your choice, roughly chopped
- 3 cups (750ml / 24 oz) of water
- 1 Tablespoon honey
- Ice

LEMONADE

INGREDIENTS
MAKES 6 TO 8 DRINKS

- 2 whole lemons
- 4 cups (1 litre / 32 oz) of water
- ¼ cup (60ml / 2 oz) maple syrup
- Ice

Ever since I bought my ©Thermomix, I make lemonade whenever we have a party. This drink is also great to take in a thermos to the beach or for a picnic. I like using whole lemons. I find the peel adds a nice flavour. My homemade lemonade became very popular at my daughter's first birthday party in California. I remember hearing the children say to each other that they had to try the lemonade! I got asked for the recipe… and here it is! I still use my ©Thermomix, as it is the only blender and food processor in my kitchen, but this recipe can be made with any blender or food processor. If you don't have a blender, juice the lemons and grate the zest and strain before serving.

1. Wash lemons, remove a bit of the top and bottom, and cut into quarters
2. Place lemons, maple syrup, and 1 cup of water in a blender or food processor
3. Pulse a few times or blend on a low setting for about 30 seconds
4. Add remaining water and stir
5. Strain lemonade through a sieve
6. Taste for sweetness and add more syrup to your liking
7. Add some ice and serve

Lemonade can be made in advance. In this case, add the ice when you're going to serve it.

I like my lemonade a bit sour, plus I don't like using lots of sugar. Try the recipe as is and make it your own by adding more sweeteners. You can also use agave syrup or honey. I find these liquid sweeteners blend easier than sugar.

I bet you will be asked to bring lemonade wherever you go!

SANGRÍA

Sangría is a very popular Spanish drink, that is easy to make and even easier to drink! There are many versions, but I have based this recipe on the one my husband used to produce with his friend and business partner Jorge. I remember when they started with the idea of making sangría that they could bottle and market. They did it and were quite successful, mainly at summer markets. You could see people walking very happily around the market. I developed and wrote this recipe as part of a wedding present for my first hairdresser in California. I wonder what she is thinking about being the first one to have it!

1. Pour the wine in a jug (pitcher) and add the lemon, orange, and apple juices. Add also the lemon and orange peels, the cinnamon sticks, maple syrup, and liquor of your choice
2. Stir to mix well and keep refrigerated for a few hours; preferably overnight
3. When ready to serve, strain the wine mixture over a big jug (pitcher) and add the lemonade. The perfect ratio is 2 parts lemonade to 1 part wine mixture. Experiment with 1 to 1 and 3 to 1 ratios, depending on how strong you like it
4. Put plenty of ice, slices of lemon and orange and fresh mint leaves

You should have enough for two large jugs (pitchers).

Enjoy (in moderation)!

INGREDIENTS
FOR 2 JUGS

- 1 bottle of red wine (Tempranillo or Pinot Noir work best)
- 4 cups (1 litre / 32 oz) bottle of sparkling lemonade (or make your own)
- Juice and peel of 1 lemon
- Juice and peel of 1 orange
- ½ cup (125ml / 4 oz) apple juice (store bought)
- 2 cinnamon sticks
- 1 to 2 shots of tequila or rum (or your favourite liquor)
- ¼ cup (60ml / 2 oz) maple syrup (or to taste)
- 1 lemon sliced
- 1 orange sliced
- Fresh mint

GOLDEN CHAI LATTE

INGREDIENTS
MAKES 4 TO 6 SERVINGS

CHAI SPICE MIX

- 1 teaspoon cardamom pods
- 1 teaspoon black pepper
- 1 star anise
- 1 teaspoon fennel seeds
- ½ cinnamon stick
- ½ teaspoon ground nutmeg
- 1 teaspoon cloves

LATTE

- 1 cup (250ml / 8 oz) milk
- 3 cups (750ml / 24 oz) of water
- 1 Tablespoon good quality black tea leaves
- 1 teaspoon Chai Spice mix
- ¼ teaspoon turmeric
- Freshly grated ginger to taste
- 1 Tablespoon honey

I have been drinking chai latte for a while. The best I remember was a cold and rainy Anzac day at a market in Melbourne, Australia, where other vendors and I braved the weather. I didn't know then that I would taste the best chai latte ever in California. I swear! My friend Maria del Mar makes the greatest chai latte. She's a very special person to me. We met before I arrived in California and we have been close friends since then. I guess the universe brought us together knowing we would get along. Luckily, both families bonded. Our husbands are best buddies, our daughters have a beautiful friendship, her little boy is our weakness and her older sons are very involved in this journey; they have created videos for me. She kindly shared her Chai recipe. Here is my version with the addition of turmeric, which makes it golden and warmer, perfect for the cold months.

CHAI SPICE MIX

1. Grind spices in a mortar and pestle or grinder
2. Mix well
3. Store in a jar

Double or triple the recipe and keep it handy in your cupboard or pantry.

LATTE

4. Place milk and water in a pot over medium heat
5. Add tea, Chai Spice, turmeric, ginger, and honey
6. Stir and bring to the boil
7. Take off the heat and let set for a couple of minutes
8. Strain well and serve while hot

This recipe is perfect for any milk of your choice, which makes it a perfect *PLANT-BASED* and or *DAIRY-FREE* drink. I particularly love it with coconut milk.

Drinks

MANGO LASSI

This is one of my favourite drinks, whether I'm eating Indian food, or I simply need a wholesome drink. I created this recipe as part of an Indian menu for a summer cooking camp that I ran at our first school in California. My assistant and I took the children on a culinary journey around the world. Although a bit eventful, the children loved the experience, the food, and learning about other cultures. I have a very fond memory of those happy faces. I received great feedback on how the children were cooking at home after their week with me and that's all it matters!

1. Peel and cut the mango
2. Place all ingredients into a powerful blender or food processor
3. Blend until you get the desired consistency
4. Add extra water for a thinner and lighter drink

You can add some ice if you like a thicker consistency.

I find the sweetness of the mango to be enough, but if you have a sweet tooth, you can add a bit of honey.

I bet this will be a regular drink in your kitchen!

INGREDIENTS
MAKES 4 DRINKS

- 2 cups natural (plain) yogurt
- 1 cup (250ml / 8 oz) of water
- 1 ripe large mango
- ½ teaspoon garam masala
- ¼ teaspoon turmeric

HOT CHOCOLATE

INGREDIENTS
MAKES 4 SERVINGS

- 1 dark chocolate bar (100gr / 3.5 oz)
- 3 cups (750ml / 24 oz) of milk
- 1 teaspoon cornstarch (cornflour) mixed with 1 Tablespoon cold milk (until well dissolved)
- ½ teaspoon ground cinnamon (optional)
- ½ teaspoon vanilla essence (extract)
- Pinch of salt
- Sugar to taste

The history of chocolate in Spain started when the Spaniards met the Cocoa (Theobroma Cacao) during the colonization of the Americas. Aztec Emperor Montezuma introduced Hernán Cortes to his favourite drink *chocolatl*, served in a golden goblet. The introduction of this ingredient to the Spanish culinary customs was certainly immediate. With this historic factor plus my experience making and serving hot chocolate at the school canteen, this recipe is a fusion of the traditional Mexican drink with a slight thickness of the Spanish favourite. I serve this hot chocolate with CHURROS (Page 58). As I am allergic to cocoa, I have relied on a group of young testers that have given me the thumbs up to the final recipe.

1. Heat milk just before boiling point
2. Reduce heat to low or simmer
3. Add chocolate, cinnamon (if using), and vanilla and stir with a wooden spoon
4. When chocolate is fully incorporated, add cornstarch mixture, salt, and sugar
5. Keep stirring until it thickens

Serve while hot and enjoy!

For a drinking hot chocolate don't add the cornstarch mixture. When the chocolate is fully incorporated, beat the drink with a hand (stick) blender to achieve a frothy cafe style drink.

Make it *PLANT-BASED* and/or *DAIRY-FREE* by using coconut milk or any alternative milk of your choice and *PLANT-BASED* chocolate.

Breakfast

"What nicer thing can you do for somebody than make them breakfast?"

ANTHONY BOURDAIN

— *Breakfast* —

YOGURT CUP

INGREDIENTS

MAKES 1 SERVE

- ½ cup yogurt (preferably natural / plain)
- ½ cup of berries (especially blueberries)
- 2 Tablespoons seeds
- Kithul syrup (or Maple)
- Ground cinnamon

I can close my eyes and be back at the school canteen making yogurt cups. We used to put glasses in muffin baking trays and make a production line to fill them up. This made it very easy to store them in the fridge before service time. They were very popular among the children, mainly during the warmer weather. This style of breakfast helped my husband on his journey to be fitter and healthier. For six months, we had a yogurt bowl with fruit and seeds for breakfast from Monday to Saturday. I joined in to support him. This recipe that I am sharing with you includes my favourite toppings and is a reasonable size breakfast. I love the softness of the fruit, the crunchiness of the seeds, and the sweetness of the syrup and cinnamon.

1. In a glass or bowl, place ¼ cup of yogurt
2. Top with ¼ cup berries, 1 Tablespoon of seeds and drizzle with syrup
3. Make a second layer using the remaining yogurt
4. Top with the rest of the berries and seeds
5. Drizzle with syrup and sprinkle ground cinnamon

This is a super breakfast! You will be full until lunchtime, or even for longer.

Kithul syrup is the perfect pairing with yogurt. Its smoky flavour takes this yogurt cup to another level. Besides, it is one of the healthiest and more sustainable sweeteners that you can use.

Make your own seeds mix. I always have a glass jar with a mix of half pumpkin seeds (*pepitas*) and half sunflower seeds. I find this works well for this yogurt cup and most salads.

CHURROS

INGREDIENTS
MAKES 4 SERVINGS

- 1 cup (150gr / 0.33 lb) plain (all-purpose) flour
- 1 teaspoon baking powder
- A pinch of salt
- 1 cup (250ml / 8 oz) of boiling water
- Light olive oil for frying

When I make churros, I always think of my dear friend Encarna. I have always loved spending time with elderly people and Encarna was one of my favourites. When I got pregnant, she made me promise that I wouldn't eat cold meats or soft cheeses. She had seen on Spanish television that it was bad for the baby. I kept my promise. I remember when I used to visit her on Thursday afternoons on my way home from work. She always had a fresh batch of delicious chicken broth ready for me and my future baby. I am sure she is looking at me from heaven and thinking that I am not making churros the way she taught me. This is my best recipe based on hers. This is a traditional Spanish churros recipe.

1. Mix the flour, baking powder, and salt in a bowl until well combined
2. Pour the boiling water over the flour mixture, stirring lightly to obtain a compact dough. You must use a wooden spoon to do this to get the best result (and not burn your hand)
3. Fill *churrera* (churros maker) or piping bag (fitted with a medium star-shaped ending) with the dough
4. Put enough oil to cover the churros in a frying pan over medium heat
5. Press down the dough and shape into drops
6. Prepare a cooling rack with kitchen paper
7. Deep fry the churros in the oil until golden and crisp, about 1 to 2 minutes per side
8. Place churros on the prepared rack until extra oil is absorbed
9. Churros should be served warm
10. You can dust them with icing (powdered) sugar for extra sweetness

Breakfast

EASY WHOLEMEAL PANCAKES

I love pancakes. I find them very tasty and rewarding to eat, plus they are super easy and quick to make. In my journey to cook healthier pancakes, I have tried many different flours. This basic recipe is a good start. If you feel confident and inspired, try using other flours. As part of my organic product range, I have a couple of pancake mixtures that I developed. You could say that I'm a pancake expert. I used to sell freshly made pancakes in markets with my beautiful helper Panta, from Thailand. I also occasionally made pancakes at the school canteen. I remember one time that I made over 100 pancakes in less than 1 hour! The children loved them, and I was very happy to cook for them. I really enjoyed it!

1. Beat the egg with the salt until pale and fluffy (this is the trick for soft and tender pancakes)
2. Add milk, oil, vanilla and mix well
3. Add flours, baking powder and mix until you get a light batter
4. Heat a griddle or non-stick pan over medium heat. Add some butter or oil and cook scoops of pancake batter in batches
5. When you see bubbles, it's time to flip them and cook for 2 more minutes

Serve pancakes with your favourite topping. At my organic kitchen, we like them with a scoop of yogurt, fresh berries, seeds, and a drizzle of syrup. Yum!

Pancakes can be made *GLUTEN-FREE* by using *buckwheat* flour. You will think you are about to eat chocolate pancakes!

For *DAIRY-FREE* use any milk of your choice and oil to cook the pancakes.

INGREDIENTS

MAKES 8 TO 10 PANCAKES

- ½ cup (75gr / 0.17 lb) wholemeal flour (can be spelt)
- ½ cup (75gr / 0.17 lb) plain (all-purpose) flour
- 2 teaspoons baking powder
- 1 whole egg
- ¾ cup (180ml / 6 oz) milk (or buttermilk; see *TIPS & TRICKS*, Page 19)
- 1 Tablespoon oil
- 1 teaspoon vanilla essence (extract)
- Pinch of salt

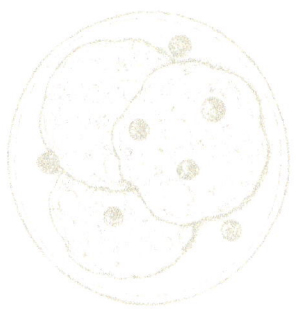

FRENCH TOAST

I wish you could see the handwritten recipe that my daughter wrote one Sunday morning that she and her friend Brooklyn decided that they would make breakfast for my hubby and me. I don't have to tell you how pleased we were! I keep that recipe as a treasure. It's gorgeous and so precise that I have used it to complete writing this recipe for you. We could hear them in the kitchen during the process. For sure, there was a bit of bossing and wrestling around – we are talking about two 11 years old girls trying to impress us! But they worked it all out and did a great job. They even set the table uniquely. If only Brooklyn would sleep over more often!

1. In a bowl, beat the eggs with the salt
2. Add milk, vanilla, and cinnamon (if using) and mix well
3. Soak the *Challah* slices until well coated
4. Heat a griddle or non-stick pan over medium heat and add some butter or oil
5. Fry *Challah* slices in batches until golden brown on both sides, for approximately 2 minutes on each side
6. Serve warm

Drizzle with your favourite syrup and sprinkle extra cinnamon, if you are a cinnamon lover like me.

As my daughter wrote in her recipe: "There you have it. Yummy French toasts!!!!!!!!!"

Although French toasts were originally made using stale bread, I like using *Challah*. I find this sweet bread makes the perfect French Toast every time. I don't add any sugar to the mixture as the bread is already sweet and I can also use it when cooking a savoury breakfast or brunch.

INGREDIENTS
MAKES 4 SERVINGS

- 8 thick slices of *Challah* bread (Page 184) or brioche
- 1 cup (250ml / 8 oz) milk
- 4 whole eggs
- 1 teaspoon vanilla essence (extract)
- Pinch of salt
- Ground cinnamon (optional)

BREAKFAST BURRITO

INGREDIENTS
MAKES 1 SERVINGS

- 1 egg
- 1 corn or wheat tortilla, depending on your preference
- ¼ cup grated cheese
- ½ medium tomato, diced
- Thin slices of ¼ avocado
- Salt & pepper to taste
- Fresh lime
- Fresh cilantro/coriander (optional)

I learned this recipe from my second kitchen mentor, Linda Wyner. I went to our local county fair in California to see her at a cooking demo. She had invited two of my students from cooking camp as her assistants. I was instantly taken by how simple and complete this recipe is for a quick bite. I have worked with Linda for three years. I have learned tons of historical food facts and cooking skills from her. The word burrito translates as *'little donkey'* from Spanish. Although its origins are unclear, burritos have become a staple in the US cuisine. Its first known reference was in Los Angeles, but the most popular type is the *Mission Burrito* originated in San Francisco.

1. Heat a non-stick pan over medium heat
2. Add some oil to the pan
3. Beat the egg with salt and pepper
4. Pour the egg and when you see that it starts to cook, place the tortilla over it and don't touch it for about 1 minute
5. Slowly, start turning the tortilla until all comes loose
6. Flip the tortilla
7. Sprinkle cheese over the middle, cover with a lid and allow to melt
8. Take the pan off the heat
9. Top the burrito with avocado and tomato
10. Squeeze a bit of fresh lime
11. Season with extra salt and pepper
12. Sprinkle fresh cilantro/coriander (if using)
13. Wrap the burrito by folding one small end of the tortilla and rolling it
14. Keep it closed with a toothpick or by wrapping it in a piece of baking (parchment) paper, and enjoy!

This is a great on the go breakfast. I also like it as lunch served with a green salad or *PERFECT WHITE RICE* (Page 138). Add *pico de gallo* or salsa instead of tomatoes, and *SIMPLE GUACAMOLE* (Page 72) instead of sliced avocado.

I'm sure it will soon be a staple in your diet.

CREPES

INGREDIENTS

MAKES 8 TO 10 CREPES

- 1 cup (250ml / 8oz) milk of your choice
- ⅔ cup (100gr / 0.22 lb) plain (all-purpose) flour
- 2 whole eggs
- 1 Tablespoon oil
- 1 teaspoon of vanilla essence (extract)
- Pinch of salt

ALTERNATIVES

The Argentinean way is to spread crepes with dulce de leche, roll, and eat them! It is a bit naughty, but truly delicious.

Go back to their origins, and make crepes *GLUTEN-FREE* using buckwheat flour.

For a *DAIRY-FREE* version, use any milk of your choice and/or water, and oil to cook them.

My family of three has a long tradition of Sunday brunches. It is a special time that we treasure. Sunday is the only morning that we can take our time cooking and enjoying being together around breakfast. For years we have alternated Pancakes, Crepes, French Toast and Churros; with Crepes being my husband's and my daughter's favourite. Crepes originate from Brittany, France, and were originally made using buckwheat flour and water. February 2nd is Crepe day in France. The date commemorates the coming of spring. According to a legend, if you hold a coin with your dominant hand and a frying pan with the other, flip a crepe and if it lands flat, your family will be prosperous that year.[4] Why don't you try it next time you're making crepes? I am sure it will be fun!

1. Place all ingredients into a bowl and whisk for 2 minutes (Use a stand or hand mixer with the whisk attachment for better results)
2. Refrigerate for 30 minutes or place in the freezer for 10 minutes (this can be done overnight or for a few hours). This resting time is very important for the batter to set. This will give you silky and scrumptious crepes
3. Whisk for a few seconds to smooth the batter before you're ready to cook
4. Heat a griddle or non-stick pan over medium heat and add some butter or oil
5. Pour or scoop the batter (approximately ¼ cup for each crepe)
6. Move the pan with a circular motion for the batter to cover the pan evenly
7. Cook crepes for about 2 minutes
8. Loosen the edges with a spatula (be careful not to break it, a crepe is very delicate)
9. Flip the crepe and cook for 1 more minute or until it is light brown
10. Stack crepes on a serving platter and keep warm by wrapping them with a clean cloth or tea towel
11. Serve warm

Crepes are usually filled or spread with sweet sauces and or fruit. You fold them twice and enjoy them with a drizzle of your favourite topping or syrup.

[4] https://epicureandculture.com/french-crepe/

Breakfast

TOMATO & SERRANO HAM TOAST

INGREDIENTS
MAKES 4 SERVINGS

- 8 slices of *PANE DI CASA BREAD* (Page 186), or any good quality bread
- 2 ripe tomatoes
- Olive oil
- 4 slices of Serrano ham

This is the most popular breakfast in Spain and one of my all times favourites. Let me tell you a story about this breakfast and my husband. When he travelled to Spain for the first time, we went to have breakfast at a local café. I ordered tomato and Serrano ham toast and he ordered a pastry. I found it strange but thought that he probably just felt like having a sweet breakfast. When my breakfast was served, you should have seen my husband's face! He looked at me and said: "How do you know about ordering this?" It was such a funny situation! But I felt bad for him, so I ordered an extra tomato & Serrano ham toast for him. Ever since, this is the first thing my husband eats when he lands in Spain. *'Pa amb tomaquet'* or *'bread with tomato'* is originally from Catalonia, but it has spread all over Spain and it is served in many restaurants and bars.

1. Heat a griddle over medium heat
2. Toast bread slices on both sides until light brown
3. Cut tomatoes in half and rub over the bread until well coated (don't throw the tomatoes away, keep them to make sauce or add to your next stew. Freeze them in a jar, and don't forget to label it!)
4. Drizzle olive oil over the bread
5. Place half slices of Serrano ham over each bread slice
6. Serve while warm

Use your toaster if it is easier for you. You can also use the oven if you are already using it for something else.

If you like the aroma of garlic, rub raw and peeled garlic over the bread before you rub the tomato.

To make it *VEGETARIAN*, leave the ham and add some salt. In fact, I usually make the *'pa amb tomaquet'* and serve the Serrano ham separately. This way, I can also enjoy having just the bread with tomato.

This is also a great appetizer and very successful to serve in the middle of your dinner table.

I hope you like it as much as my hubby and I do!

— Small Bites —

The recipes in this section are some of my favourite snacks. They make a perfect *TAPAS* banquet. Choose one of the dips and between *TORTILLA* and *ZUCCHINI SLICE*, as they are both egg-based recipes. I promise your guests will be delighted with the combinations of flavours.

You will also have dishes for all food allergies, intolerances, and preferences. You can even change them following my comments at the end of the recipes or adding your own touches. I can picture how beautiful your table will look and how amazing your kitchen will smell! When is your next *TAPAS* night? And don't forget to add some '*pa amb tomaquet*'! (Page 65).

Small Bites

"The willingness and ability to live fully in the now eludes many people. While eating your appetizer, don't be concerned with dessert."

WAYNE DYER

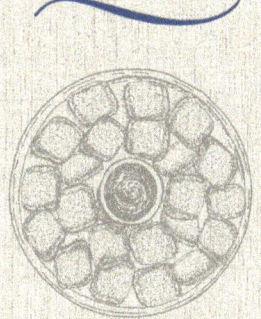

FETA & AVOCADO DIP

INGREDIENTS

MAKES 1 ½ CUPS

- 1 medium to large ripe avocado
- 75gr (0.17 lb / 2.65 oz) feta cheese
- 1 Tablespoon lemon juice
- ½ teaspoon ground cumin
- ½ teaspoon dry oregano
- 1 Tablespoon extra virgin olive oil
- ¼ teaspoon salt, or to taste
- Ground black pepper

My friend Nina made this dip for me one day and served it over bread for a light lunch. She made it so quickly I was truly impressed. I visited her after a hairdresser session near her house. She is a wonderful cook and one of the most adorable women I know. Nina is beautiful too, and a super mum and wife. We have been mistaken for sisters many times. It may be our curly long hair and our European vibes. She was my maid of honour and witness at my wedding. As with most recipes in this book, this is my version of her original mashed avocado and feta on toast. It is one of my favourite dips, but sadly, not for my husband.

1. Mash the avocado in a bowl
2. Crumble the feta cheese and mix with the avocado
3. Add lemon and oil and stir, followed by the spices and mix well
4. Season with salt and pepper
5. Taste and adjust the seasoning to your liking

Serve over toasted *PANE DI CASA* (page 186) or as part of an appetizer (antipasto) platter.

PERFECT HUMMUS

My dear friend Panayota introduced me to hummus. We used to work together, but our friendship grew around food, my Spanish culture, and her Cypriot background. I have learned most of what I know about Greek food from her. Her spanakopita is the best! She was the first person to encourage me to apply for my Australian citizenship. My response to her was that I would do it when I had an Australian baby. So, one day I went to work and told her that I was going to apply to be Australian. She understood that I was expecting; what a beautiful moment that was! My daughter has been very fortunate to have women like Panayota to be part of her childhood.

1. In a mortar and pestle put salt, peppercorns, and garlic and pound until it forms a smooth paste. This will infuse the garlic flavour over the entire dip more evenly
2. Strain chickpeas (garbanzo beans) over a bowl and reserve the liquid
3. Place the ingredients in a food processor in the following order: chickpeas (garbanzo beans), tahini paste, garlic paste, cumin, paprika, lemon, and olive oil
4. Process hummus until you achieve a smooth consistency. If it is too dry, add 1 to 2 Tablespoons of the beans water; one at a time
5. When you are happy with the texture of the dip, taste for seasoning
6. To serve, plate on a pretty bowl and sprinkle with extra paprika and a drizzle of olive oil

I always serve my hummus with carrot and celery sticks and plain crackers.

To make this recipe with dry chickpeas, soak 150gr (5oz) dry garbanzo beans overnight. Strain and cook over medium heat for 1 to 1.5 hours until tender. Let them cool and then proceed as per the recipe.

Use any beans that you like or you have in your pantry. I really like pinto beans hummus. The same way, use sunflower seed paste instead of tahini. Don't discard the *'aquafaba'*, chickpeas (garbanzo) water. It is the perfect substitute for egg whites in *PLANT-BASED* recipes.

INGREDIENTS
MAKES 1 ½ CUPS

- 1 tin (can) 425gr (15 oz) chickpeas (garbanzo beans)
- 2 Tablespoons Tahini paste
- 1 garlic clove
- 1 ½ teaspoon ground cumin
- 1 teaspoon Spanish smoked paprika, plus extra for topping
- Juice and zest (rind) of 1 lemon (start with ½ and taste)
- ¼ cup (60ml / 2 oz) extra virgin olive oil
- ½ teaspoon salt, or to taste
- 4 black peppercorns

SIMPLE GUACAMOLE

INGREDIENTS

MAKES 1 ½ CUPS

- 2 ripe avocados
- 1 garlic clove
- ½ teaspoon ground cumin
- ½ teaspoon Spanish smoked paprika, plus extra for topping
- ¼ teaspoon cayenne pepper (or more if you like spicy flavours)
- 1 Tablespoon lime juice
- 1 Tablespoon olive oil
- ½ teaspoon salt, or to taste
- 6 black peppercorns
- 1 handful roughly chopped fresh coriander (cilantro) to garnish

Mexicans combined the Aztec words for avocado and sauce, 'aguacate' and 'mole', to make guacamole. Although I had eaten guacamole before, it wasn't until I was introduced to my husband's family, that I began to eat it frequently. My lovely in-laws always receive you with what they call 'picada', a platter with nibbles, including guacamole. Whenever we went to visit them, we always enjoyed a 'picada' with a glass of wine and great conversation around their table. My husband started making guacamole and added cooked garlic for extra flavour. When I started cooking Mexican food I began experimenting with my own guacamole, this recipe is my favourite combination of flavours. I hope you like it and make it as frequently as we do.

1. In a mortar and pestle put salt, peppercorns, and garlic and pound until it forms a smooth paste
2. Place avocados in the mortar bowl and mash with the pestle to your desire consistency. I like semi smooth guacamole
3. Add spices, lime juice, and olive oil
4. Mix well and taste for seasoning
5. Sprinkle with extra paprika and cayenne pepper
6. Garnish with cilantro (coriander)

Serve in the mortar bowl over a platter with corn chips (totopos).

This guacamole keeps in the fridge for a couple of days. Drizzle extra lime or lemon juice to prevent from going dark and cover well.

Use lemon instead of lime juice and dry oregano instead of fresh coriander (cilantro).

CUCUMBER, GOAT CHEESE & SMOKED SALMON CANAPE

I love high tea. I really enjoy the single-bite food spread that comes with it. I made my own high tea for my birthday celebration with my Californian book club ladies. I had to make sure that at least half of the bites were *GLUTEN-FREE*, so the lovely Estelle could enjoy eating and tasting my food. She's an expat like me, most of us are. It is incredible, and at the same time beautiful, how we support each other. This particular canapé was created by chance from the concept of smoked salmon, cream cheese, and cucumber sandwich. I remembered I had some leftover smoked salmon in the fridge, I found cucumber and thought that goat cheese would give more flavour. Garnished with fresh dill from fennel and voila! Not only Estelle enjoyed them, but we all also did.

1. Cut both ends of the cucumber, diagonally
2. If the skin is tough, peel the cucumber in a stripe pattern
3. Slice cucumber with a mandolin, through a thicker setting than making round potato chips
4. Place cucumber slices on a serving platter
5. Spread a thick coat of goat cheese on each slice
6. Place a piece of smoked salmon over the cheese to cover the canapé
7. Garnish with fresh dill

Délicieux!

Image on page 66

INGREDIENTS

MAKES 15 CANAPÉS

- 1 large fresh cucumber
- 113gr (0.25 lb / 4 oz) smoked salmon
- 226gr (0.5 lb / 8 oz) goat cheese
- Fresh dill to garnish

CHORIZO & MELTED MANCHEGO TAPA

INGREDIENTS

MAKES 15 TAPAS

- 15 slices *PANE DI CASA* bread (page 186)
- 1 Spanish chorizo sausage
- 250gr (0.6 lb / approximately 8 oz) wedge of Manchego cheese
- Olive oil

I remember eating this tapa in a Spanish restaurant in Melbourne, Australia many years ago. We were a big group of friends from all corners of the world, something very common in Melbourne. My friend Karen organised it. She loves Spanish food! I met Karen at an English preparatory course before I started my MBA. We have been friends ever since. I loved the combination of chorizo and Manchego cheese flavour so much that it became part of my regular tapas menu. Besides, it always brings me happy memories of that night when I tasted it for the first time.

1. Preheat the oven to 200C (400F)
2. Cut the bread as if you were making toasts, about 1.5cm thick (0.60")
3. Prepare a baking tray (sheet pan) with baking (parchment) paper
4. Place bread slices on the baking tray (sheet pan)
5. Drizzle or brush the bread with olive oil
6. Slice chorizo diagonally, about 0.5cm thick (¼" approximately)
7. Put a couple of slices of chorizo over each slice of bread
8. Slice Manchego cheese also 0.5cm thick (¼" approximately)
9. Place Manchego slices over chorizo
10. Bake for 5 minutes, checking to make sure the Manchego doesn't dry out
11. Serve on a nice wooden board or your favourite serving platter

This is a nice snack or even breakfast. I love eating the leftover cheese and chorizo (don't tell anyone!).

You can also use store bought baguette or other bread of your choice, but make sure it is thick in the inside to soak the oils that both the chorizo and Manchego release.

For a *VEGETARIAN* option, omit the chorizo and sprinkle a bit of smoked paprika over the cheese.

— *Small Bites* —

AUSSIE SAUSAGE ROLLS

A ustralians love sausage rolls. You can find them in every bakery and many cafes. A traditional British meal, it is very popular in the Commonwealth. It's also a great party food. I started making sausage rolls for my daughter's 4th birthday party. That's when I started catering for every event that I organised.

The need to know what's in the food that we eat has made me a total hands-on foodie. Ever since I arrived in California, I have made sausage rolls using turkey thigh mince. It's a healthier and more sustainable option over here.

My daughter loves them!

1. Place pastry on a lightly floured clean bench
2. Roll pastry, if needed, until you have 4 square sheets of approximately 24 x 24cm (9.44" x 9.44")

AUSSIE SAUSAGE ROLLS (continued)

3. Peel and roughly cut carrots and onion, place them in a food processor with the spinach and pulse until they are finely chopped
4. Add this mixture to the meat, together with the *GARLIC & PARSLEY BLEND*, salt, Tamari sauce, and pepper
5. Now, get your hands dirty and mix well until all ingredients are well combined (get the children to do it; they love it!). You can also do this using a stand mixer with the paddle attachment. This is the way I do it.
6. Slice each sheet of pastry in half
7. Divide the mince mixture into 8 equal portions, for each puff pastry
8. Place a portion of the mixture in the middle of the long edge of the pastry and shape into a long sausage
9. Slightly beat the egg with 1 Tablespoon of water
10. Brush the sides of the pastry with egg and roll pastry over to cover the mince
11. Do this as firmly as possible, without breaking the puff pastry, and seal by pressing the edges with your fingers. You can also use a fork
12. Cut each roll into 4 equal pieces
13. Place them on trays laid with baking (parchment) paper leaving space for the pastry to puff
14. Brush the top of the rolls with the egg and water mixture and prick with a fork
15. Preheat the oven to 200C (400F)
16. Bake sausage rolls for 20 to 25 minutes until the pastry is puffy and golden and filling is cooked through
17. I like turning them around after 15 minutes so that both sides are golden and puffy
18. Let them rest for 5 minutes before serving

Traditionally, sausage rolls are served with tomato sauce (ketchup) to dip them into. Top with sesame or poppy seeds. They look and taste great!

Experiment and make them *VEGETARIAN*: fill them with a mixture of spinach, green/spring onions (scallions), ricotta, feta cheese, and eggs with plenty of seasoning. You will have the full party covered!

Sausage rolls freeze really well. Make sure you thaw them before baking.

INGREDIENTS
(MAKES 32 SMALL ROLLS OR 16 LUNCH SIZE)

- 4 square sheets frozen puff pastry (165gr / 0.36 lb / 5.8 oz each)
- 2 medium carrots
- 1 medium brown onion
- 1 Tablespoon *GARLIC & PARSLEY BLEND* (Page 32)
- 1 cup spinach leaves
- 1kg (2.2 lb) ground turkey (or chicken)
- 1 Tablespoon Tamari sauce (or soy)
- ½ teaspoon salt
- Freshly ground black pepper
- 1 egg

TORTILLA (SPANISH OMELETTE)

INGREDIENTS
MAKES 6 TO 8 SERVINGS

- 6 eggs
- 1kg (2.2 lb) potatoes
- 1 medium zucchini (courgette)
- 1 large brown onion
- 1 teaspoon salt
- Freshly ground black pepper
- Light olive oil for frying

The humble *Tortilla* is one of the cuisine symbols of Spain. It can range from authentic and basic ingredients to non-traditional preparations with many additional ingredients. There's the controversy about whether it has to include onion or not. I like it with onion and the addition of zucchini makes this recipe super tasty, soft, and delicious! Tortilla is a perfect *VEGETARIAN* meal. It is my friend Catherine's favourite meal. The one she always asked me to make whenever we ate together. I met Catherine at work and we quickly became acquainted. We have read together for more than ten years. We have shared many happy and also sad moments. I owe my first cat, Goldie, to Catherine. She and her family have played an important part in my life in Melbourne, Australia. They helped me organise my mother's memorial. It was such a beautiful celebration! I will be forever grateful.

1. Peel the potatoes, cut them in fourths vertically, and slice them thinly. I use a mandolin with a medium setting for this. It's easier and quicker and it ensures all potatoes are the same size and will cook at the same time
2. Peel the zucchini, cut in half vertically, and slice as per potatoes
3. Peel the onion, cut in half from the top, and slice thinly
4. Using a cast iron or deep frying pan, heat enough oil to fry the potatoes, zucchini, and onion over medium-high heat
5. Add ½ teaspoon salt and freshly ground black pepper into the vegetables and mix well
6. Place potatoes mixture in the hot oil and bring to the boil. Reduce heat to medium and fry for approximately 10 minutes, until potatoes are soft and cooked through, stirring occasionally (do not brown the potatoes)
7. Prepare a colander over a bowl or dip plate
8. Strain potatoes mixture with the help of a slotted spoon over the colander and let set until most of the oil has dripped (this will make your tortilla less oily)

TORTILLA (SPANISH OMELETTE) (continued)

9. Separate the egg whites and beat them with the remaining ½ teaspoon salt until foamy. You can use a stand or hand mixer to do this, but we're not looking for meringue. (This is the secret to my soft and juicy tortilla)
10. Start adding the yolks, one at a time, until all the eggs are well mixed and fluffy
11. Add potato mixture to the eggs and gently fold until well combined
12. Prepare a non-stick 25 to 30cm (10" to 12") pan to cook the tortilla
13. Heat enough oil, approximately 1 Tablespoon, to cover the pan when heated. We don't want our tortilla to stick
14. Pour eggs and potatoes mixture over the pan, shake to settle, and cook over medium heat for 5 minutes, until golden brown
15. Now we need to flip the tortilla to cook it on the other side. Use a platter bigger than the pan and flip over. With the help of a spatula, slip back the tortilla into the pan on the uncooked side. Gather all edges to make a perfect 'cake' and cook 5 extra minutes
16. Your tortilla is now ready to be eaten!

Tortilla tastes very nice eaten at room temperature or even cold. It makes a perfect picnic meal.

I like making it for dinner and serve it with a salad and *MAYONNAISE* (Page 35).

Cut tortilla in 16 wedges and serve over *TOMATO BREAD* (Page 65). Put a slice of roasted red pepper over the tortilla wedge for fancier plating or as an appetizer or *tapas banquet*.

HALLOUMI & WATERMELON SLICES

Halloumi cheese has been said to originate in Cyprus. It was initially made during the Medieval Byzantine period. Halloumi became popular in the rest of the Middle East region. It's a semi-hard, unripened, and brined cheese with a high melting point. Grilled Halloumi is delicious in salads and served with vegetables. Having worked with Cyprians for many years, I have been lucky to try homemade halloumi. I know the 'real deal'! This Cypriot recipe is very fresh, perfect for summer as a snack or dessert. Νόστιμο!

1. Cut watermelon in 4 and slice into triangle shape pieces
2. Remove skin and place on a serving platter
3. Slice halloumi cheese from the short edge
4. Place a slice of halloumi over each slice of watermelon
5. Garnish with fresh mint leaves
6. Serve and enjoy!

This is a perfect picnic food and also for lunch boxes.

Halloumi cheese is not easily replaceable, however you can use feta and also mexican style panela cheese for this recipe.

INGREDIENTS

MAKES 4 TO 6 SERVINGS

- 250gr (0.55 lb / 8.8 oz) halloumi cheese
- ½ small seeded red watermelon
- Fresh mint leaves

ZUCCHINI SLICE

I discovered this dish thanks to my long term client, Helen. I used to work in their home office for many years. They're one of the nicest families I know. One day, the smell from her kitchen filled the office and I went to see what she was cooking. She told me about zucchini slice and explained briefly how to make it. Of course, I went to my kitchen and experimented making it my own way. I taught my niece Mayte in Spain how to make it and I'm aware she has passed the recipe to other people as well. I cook it at least once a month. It is a complete meal served with a salad. I love it for lunch and it's also great picnic food.

1. Grate zucchini and carrots
2. Thinly chop the onion (you can do the grating and chopping with the help of a food processor)
3. Slice the bacon in thin strips from the narrow side
4. In a large bowl, beat eggs with the salt and pepper
5. Add grated vegetables, onion, bacon, cheese, flour, and oil to the egg mixture and fold until well combined
6. Grease a 30 x 22 x 5cm (13" x 9" x 2 ¼") baking tray or cake pan and pour slice mixture. (You can also use a cast-iron pan)
7. Preheat the oven to 200C (400F)
8. Bake slice for 30 to 40 minutes
9. Check if the slice is fully cooked by inserting a knife. If it comes clean, it's cooked
10. Let rest for 10 to 15 minutes before serving

I haven't indicated any type of flour as this slice works with any flour that you want to use. This gives you the freedom to make it *GLUTEN-FREE* or to use alternative flours: spelt, besan, lentils, rice. You can also omit the bacon for a *VEGETARIAN* version.

To serve as an appetizer or as part of a *TAPAS banquet*, cut into bite-size squares or use your favourite cookie cutters. This is a great idea for special celebrations.

INGREDIENTS
MAKES 6 TO 8 SERVINGS

- 3 medium to large zucchinis (courgettes)
- 1 large carrot (or 2 medium)
- 1 medium brown onion
- 4 rashers (slices) of bacon
- 1 cup (100gr / 0.22 lb) grated cheddar cheese (or similar)
- 1 cup (150gr / 0.33 lb) flour
- ½ cup (125ml / 4 oz) extra virgin olive oil
- 1 Tablespoon *GARLIC & PARSLEY BLEND* (Page 32)
- 6 eggs
- 1 teaspoon salt
- Freshly ground black pepper to taste

EMPANADAS (dough)

INGREDIENTS

FOR THE DOUGH:
(MAKES 15 TO 20 EMPANADAS)

- 1 + ⅔ cups (250gr / 0.55 lbs / 8.8 oz) plain (all-purpose) flour
- 1 teaspoon baking powder
- 50gr (4 Tablespoons) cold butter
- ⅓ + ⅛ cup (100ml / 3.38 oz) water
- 2 teaspoons lemon juice
- ½ teaspoon salt
- 1 whole egg

I made *empanadas* for the first time when my daughter started school. We had to contribute food for a gathering and I thought that sharing a bit of our family culture with our class would be nice. I watched my lovely mother-in-law Reyna make empanadas countless times. She's such a natural and her empanadas are so delicious that I always felt intimidated to make them myself. I am glad I started making them. I usually get asked to bring them when I go to a party. This recipe was completed when my husband's parents came to visit us in California to celebrate our daughter's birthday. Knowing that her grandparents were coming, she requested a party with empanadas and *argentinian asado*. Reyna and I got to work and created this wonderful dough. I also learned the trick about mixing the olives with the filling to increase saltiness and flavour. Two women sharing their recipes and cooking with love.

1. Place flour, baking powder, and salt in a food processor and pulse a couple of times, or whisk by hand in a bowl
2. Add chilled butter cut into small cubes and process until it resembles fine breadcrumbs. To do this by hand, rub the butter into the flour mixture using the tip of your fingers. Children love doing this, but keep an eye on them so that they don't over melt the butter
3. Add egg, lemon juice, and water and pulse until dough is formed; or mix by hand
4. Place the dough on a floured surface and knead until soft and homogeneous. (You can also use a stand mixer to make the dough from the start, using the dough hook attachment)
5. Wrap the dough with a tea towel and place in the fridge for at least ½ hour, or until the filling is at room temperature
6. Roll the dough out onto a floured surface, or between 2 sheets of parchment (baking) paper, and cut in circles using a small plate, bowl, or a large cookie cutter (about 12cm / 4.5" in diameter)
7. Empanada dough discs can be frozen for later use. Place a piece of parchment (baking) paper between each disc to avoid sticking

EMPANADAS (filling)

INGREDIENTS

FOR THE FILLING

- 500gr (1.1 lb) minced (ground) beef
- 1 medium yellow (brown) onion
- 3 spring / green onions (scallions)
- 2 garlic cloves
- 2 medium tomatoes
- 2 potatoes
- 2 carrots
- 1 teaspoon maple syrup
- 2 teaspoons dry oregano
- ¼ teaspoon ground cayenne pepper (or more to taste)

This recipe makes double what you need for the dough, I find it nice to have extra and freeze it so next time I only have to make the dough. You can also make a meat pie using the dough from *EMPANADA GALLEGA* (Page 156).

1. Heat 1 Tablespoon of oil in a shallow saucepan over medium heat
2. Cook meat until browned and reserve (you can do this in batches)
3. Chop onions, garlic, and tomatoes
4. Heat the remaining Tablespoon of oil and gently sauté onions and garlic with the tomatoes for 2 to 3 minutes
5. Peel the potatoes and carrots and cut into small cubes
6. Add potatoes and carrots to the pan and stir well
7. Add spices, one at a time, including maple syrup, and mix well every time
8. Pour stock (broth) and cook for 15 minutes or until the vegetables are tender. (Omit the meat and you'll have *VEGETARIAN* empanadas)
9. Return the meat to the saucepan and cook for 5 extra minutes
10. Finely chop the olives, add to the filling mixture and stir to combine
11. Let cool down to room temperature

EMPANADAS (assemble)

TO ASSEMBLE THE EMPANADAS:

1. Chop the hard-boiled eggs and place in a bowl
2. Beat 1 egg yolk with 1 Tablespoon of water and use the egg white to seal the empanadas
3. Place 1 to 2 Tablespoons of filling and 1 teaspoon of hard-boiled egg in the middle of a dough disc. Don't overfill them, it's easier to seal empanadas with less filling
4. Brush egg white around the edge of the disc
5. Fold the dough, seal well and brush with the egg yolk and water mixture
6. Repeat for all empanadas
7. Bake at 200C (400F) for 20 to 25 minutes, until golden brown
8. You can also deep-fry the empanadas. This is the traditional way in Córdoba, Argentina, where my husband was born. These are juicer and the juice is part of the fun eating them!

Empanadas can be made in advance. I find that they cook (and taste) better if I have them in the fridge for 1 day or overnight. Always cover them with a tea towel and take out of the fridge while the oven is preheating.

In my cooking classes, we cook the filling with the vegetables only, using vegetable stock (broth). We then cook the meat in a separate pan. This way we cover all the students' food preferences. Do the same when you have a party and change the design of the sealing. For instance, you can seal the vegetarian empanadas using a fork, so you can differentiate them from the meat ones.

Serve them with *CHIMICHURRI* (Page 178); it adds a great depth of flavour. Although not traditionally Argentinean, I tried this at a restaurant in Melbourne, Australia and I liked it.

INGREDIENTS

FOR THE FILLING
CONTINUED

- 2 teaspoons ground cumin
- 1 teaspoon ground Spanish smoked paprika
- Salt & pepper to taste
- 1 cup (250ml / 8oz) chicken or vegetable stock (broth; or more if needed)
- 2 Tablespoons olive oil
- 2 hard-boiled eggs
- 12 stuffed green olives (6 if they're giant)
- 1 egg

SMOKED SALMON & FENNEL CROQUETTE

Traditionally these crispy and creamy bites were made with leftover meat from 'pucheros' and stews, and using old bread as breadcrumbs. Today croquettes have all different types of fillings and are served as a delicacy in many restaurants and bars across Spain and the world. I presented this recipe in a contest among other Spaniards in a Spain National Day celebration in Melbourne, Australia. I didn't win, but I keep a very fond memory of the event as I took my dear friend Luisa with me. She's my Australian *mother*. We are both from Córdoba, Spain, although she immigrated to Australia many years before me. She always makes croquettes the old traditional way and I have enjoyed numerous sessions of shaping and eating her delicious 'croquetas'.

1. Finely chop onion and fennel (this can be done with a food processor)
2. Heat a heavy bottom pan or pot over medium heat and add oil and butter. Sauté fennel, stirring occasionally for 5 minutes
3. Add onion and stir fry for 5 more minutes
4. Cook flour with the fennel and onion stirring constantly, for about 1 minute
5. Pour milk, a little at a time, making sure to mix well
6. Add smoked salmon and season with salt and pepper
7. Bring mixture to a boil, stirring constantly, until it thickens
8. Scrape the croquette mixture onto a shallow dish and let cool to room temperature
9. Cover with a tea towel or lid and refrigerate for at least 4 hours
10. Beat eggs with the reserved Tablespoon of milk in a shallow bowl
11. Place breadcrumbs on another shallow bowl
12. Divide croquette mixture into a Tablespoon size and roll into an oval shape
13. Dip each croquette in the egg mixture, then in the breadcrumbs, until well coated. Place on a platter

INGREDIENTS
MAKES APPROXIMATELY 32 CROQUETTES

- 200gr (0.44 lb / 8 oz) smoked salmon, finely chopped
- 1 small fennel bulb, white part only
- 1 medium brown onion
- 6 Tablespoons plain (all-purpose) flour
- 2 cups (500ml / 16 oz) milk, reserving 1 Tablespoon
- 1 Tablespoon olive oil
- 1 Tablespoon butter
- ¼ teaspoon nutmeg
- Salt and pepper to taste
- Breadcrumbs
- 2 whole eggs
- Light olive oil for deep frying

SMOKED SALMON & FENNEL CROQUETTE
(continued)

14. In a saucepan, heat oil for frying until shimmering. You can test if the oil is ready by frying a piece of stale bread. That's how my mother used to do it and I loved eating the *'toston'*, fried bread
15. Prepare a wire rack over a tray and cover with kitchen paper
16. Fry croquettes in batches, being very gentle not to break them, for about 2 minutes each side, until they are golden brown
17. Transfer fried croquettes to the prepared rack
18. Serve while warm

Croquettes can be made up to 2 days in advance. In fact, for better results, keep them in the fridge overnight.

Croquettes pair very well with *MAYONNAISE* (Page 35). They can be served as part of a tapas banquet. I like serving them as dinner with a bowl of light soup and a salad.

Make it *DAIRY- FREE* by substituting the milk for any non-dairy milk of your choice.

Experiment with *GLUTEN-FREE* flour. You may need less liquid, so start with 1 ½ cups of milk to achieve a playable thickness. Also, use *GLUTEN-FREE* breadcrumbs.

For a *VEGETARIAN* version, use finely chopped carrots and fry them with the fennel.

Make them *PLANT-BASED* using your favourite non-dairy milk instead of eggs to dip the croquettes, and olive oil instead of butter.

I usually make a double batch and freeze them for later use. Place *'croquetas'* on a tray lined up with baking (parchment) paper; cover and freeze them overnight. The next day, place all croquetas in a bag and you will have them ready to enjoy anytime! Croquetas fry much better when they're cold.

Salads & Vegetable Side Dishes

"I make an enormous amount of salads, but my salads are like meals. I like going down to the farmers' market and looking to see whatever you can find, because you can put anything in a salad."

ANDY MACDOWELL

PICADILLO SALAD

Picadillo is a very traditional summer salad from my hometown Córdoba, Spain. I chose this salad to represent Spanish cuisine in my summer cooking camp at our first school in California. My sister Rosa, who is not a kitchen lover like me, makes a delicious *picadillo*. Traditionally this salad does not have olives, but my sister adds them to hers and I love it! I really like the combination of the colour green and red and the different textures. This salad can be made into a whole meal, adding some canned tuna or steam white fish. Don't forget to use the olive oil from the tuna tin (can) to make the dressing. This will give extra flavour to your salad.

1. Cut the onion into 4 wedges and thinly slice it from bottom to top
2. Macerate the onion with the lemon juice from the dressing
3. Cut tomatoes into thin, small wedges
4. Slice the green capsicums (bell peppers) into bite-size strips
5. Place all ingredients into a salad bowl
6. Complete the dressing with the olive oil, salt, and pepper and mix well
7. Serve in the middle of the table and enjoy!

The traditional recipe uses Italian style green peppers.

I like using cherry or mini grape tomatoes. I prefer their sweeter flavour, plus they have the perfect bite-size when cut in half.

If you use giant green stuffed olives, cut them in half.

INGREDIENTS
MAKES 4 TO 6 SERVINGS

- 2 large tomatoes
- 2 green capsicums (bell peppers)
- 1 small red onion
- ¼ cup green stuffed Spanish olives
- Lemon dressing (Page 39)

GREEN SALAD

INGREDIENTS

MAKES 4 TO 6 SERVINGS

- 1 head of butter lettuce
- 1 medium to large cucumber
- 1 large avocado
- Aceto dressing (Page 39)

I made this salad as a contribution to our second Thanksgiving dinner in California. To my surprise, Ethan, our friends' son, almost ate it all by himself! His mum felt bad, but I really liked seeing him enjoying it so much. We don't know if it was the dressing, the cucumber, which he really likes, or the combination of all the flavours. Ethan is a very special boy. His sister Mirella is one of my daughter's best friends. They have amazing parents. I always think of Ethan when I make this salad.

1. Wash lettuce and tear the leaves into bite-size pieces
2. Peel cucumber in stripes, cut in half lengthways, deseed and slice thinly
3. Cut avocado in half and cut into thin slices
4. Prepare the salad in layers in this order: lettuce, cucumber, lettuce, avocado, lettuce, cucumber, lettuce, avocado, or until you run out of ingredients
5. Drizzle the Aceto dressing over the salad and serve

This salad complements many main meals. I like serving it with *ARGENTINIAN ASADO* (Page 175) and *BUTTERFLY LEMON & ROSEMARY CHICKEN* (Page 172).

If you can't find butter lettuce, use any other green lettuce of your choice. I prefer butter lettuce for its vibrant colour, tender leaves, and great flavour.

CUCUMBER & FRESH MINT SALAD

I clearly owe this salad to my dear friend Carla. She always made cucumber salad when we went to her house for dinner. Sometimes we only went for a visit, but always ended up staying until late. My daughter and her son Bruno were born 3 days apart. We shared our pregnancy and many special moments together. She was a great help during my first year as a new mum. My daughter was always happy to stay at her house. In fact, she would not stay anywhere else whenever my husband and I had a date. I miss our confident chats and our afternoons knitting and drinking coffee while our children played happily. One day you look around and realize that you have formed your own family. That happens with your friends when you live overseas.

1. Peel the cucumber in stripes, cut in half lengthways, deseed and cut into 0.5cm (0.2") slices (you don't need to peel if you use Persian or English cucumbers)
2. Wash the mint leaves and dry thoroughly with a tea towel (or spin dry using a salad spinner)
3. Place cucumber slices in a salad bowl
4. Tear the mint leaves and sprinkle over the cucumber
5. Drizzle with the lemon dressing

I like the crunchiness and freshness of this salad.

Cucumber salad goes really well with *DAHL* (Page 125).

You can add goat cheese or crumble some feta cheese for extra flavour and texture.

(*) Photo on page 165

INGREDIENTS
MAKES 4 SERVINGS

- 2 large cucumbers
- 1 big handful of fresh mint leaves
- Lemon dressing (Page 39)

LETTUCE, MANCHEGO, APPLE, BLACK OLIVES & WALNUT SALAD

This is my favourite salad by far. I really enjoy the combination of ingredients. Take a piece of each ingredient and you will have an explosion of flavour in your mouth! I first ate this salad at a Spanish restaurant in Melbourne, Australia. My friend Karen came with her partner to visit. While the boys went to the footy (AFL: Australian Football League), I organised a girls night out. This was the second time Karen came back to Australia. I always found time to catch up with her. I very much enjoy her company. She's lovely, very talented with languages and loves Spanish food!

1. Wash lettuce thoroughly and tear the leaves to bite-size pieces
2. Cut the apple in half from the stem, core, cut in quarters, and slice thinly. You can use a mandolin or slicer for this task, this way you will have even pieces
3. Cut Manchego cheese into cubes
4. Place lettuce leaves on a shallow salad bowl
5. Top with apple slices, Manchego cubes, olives, and walnuts
6. Drizzle the Aceto dressing over the salad and serve

I like serving this salad with *SEAFOOD PAELLA* (Page 139) or *BAKED TROUT WITH SERRANO HAM* (Page 160).

I eat it for lunch during the warmer months. I find it makes a full and satisfying meal.

A comer!

INGREDIENTS

MAKES 4 TO 6 SERVINGS

- 4 large handfuls of lettuce, I like using purple romaine (cos) or any red leaf lettuce
- 1 apple (preferably a sweet variety: Gala, Fuji or Golden Delicious)
- 125gr (about ¼ lb) Manchego cheese
- 16 black olives
- 2 handfuls of roasted walnuts
- Aceto dressing (Page 39)

SPINACH, KALAMATA OLIVES & RICOTTA SALAD

INGREDIENTS

MAKES 4 TO 6 SERVINGS

- 4 large handfuls of spinach leaves
- 24 Kalamata olives
- ¼ cup fresh ricotta cheese
- Lemon dressing (Page 39)

I started eating raw spinach leaves in Australia. I had never seen baby or loose spinach leaves before. I remember making this salad for my friend Nickie for lunch. She loves salads and I invented this one for the two of us. She loved it! I like how the ricotta blends after the salad is tossed, creating a creamy and thick dressing. During one of our Spanish holidays, my husband cooked an *Argentinian Asado* for my family. I served this salad and all the women commented on how delicious and different it was. I wonder why salads are more appreciated by women.

1. Wash spinach leaves in a bowl with water and a drizzle of white vinegar
2. Rinse and gently dry leaves with a tea towel or using a salad spinner
3. Cut olives in half from the top
4. Place spinach leaves in a salad bowl
5. Top with olives and small teaspoons of ricotta
6. Drizzle with the lemon dressing, toss and serve

Deliciosa!

RAINBOW BEETROOT CARPACCIO WITH GOAT CHEESE & FRESH CILANTRO

Beetroot is one of my favourite vegetables. I made this salad for the first time one night that I hadn't organised dinner. Yes, this happens to me too... When my husband and I got home we looked at what we had in the fridge. We quickly improvised dinner with chicken and beetroot. One hour later we were sitting at the dinner table enjoying a delicious and healthy meal. I love it when my husband and I work as a team in the kitchen! We both agreed that if we had ordered food, we wouldn't have eaten earlier. I hope this story empowers you to improvise and be creative in the kitchen before you consider ordering food.

1. Brush beetroot in a bowl with water and a dash of white vinegar
2. Place beetroot in a casserole, cover with water and 1 teaspoon salt
3. Bring the beets to a boil and simmer for 20 to 25 minutes
4. Insert a small knife to check if the beetroot is tender
5. Rinse beetroot in cold water and peel when they are cool enough to handle (you can also put them in an ice bath to speed up this step)
6. Thinly slice beetroot using a mandolin or slicer
7. Plate salad by overlaying beetroot slices, interchanging the colours until all platter is covered
8. Top with small pieces of goat cheese
9. Scatter cilantro (coriander) leaves
10. Drizzle the Aceto dressing over the salad and serve

This is a great *PLANT-BASED* dish if you serve the cheese in a separate bowl.

Yum!

INGREDIENTS
MAKES 4 TO 6 SERVINGS

- 2 medium red beetroots
- 2 medium golden beetroots
- 125gr (about ¼ lb) fresh goat cheese
- 1 handful fresh cilantro (coriander) leaves
- Aceto dressing (Page 39)

ROASTED BEETROOT, SWEET POTATO & SEEDS SALAD

INGREDIENTS

MAKES 4 TO 6 SERVINGS

- 500gr (1.1 lb) beetroot
- 500gr (1.1 lb) sweet potato
- 4 good handfuls mixed lettuce
- 3 Tablespoons seeds of your choice (I like 50/50 roasted sunflower and pumpkin seeds)
- 2 Tablespoons olive oil
- 1 teaspoon salt
- Pepper
- Aceto dressing (Page 39)

For this recipe, I was inspired at a potluck Christmas party in a yacht. Fancy right? We sailed along Port Phillip Bay in Melbourne, Australia. It is summer at Christmas time in the Southern Hemisphere, but I remember it being cold and very windy… typical Melbourne weather! It was a lovely experience and I got to know my co-workers in a more personal way. This is my husband's favourite salad. He always says he will be happy to eat it every day.

1. Preheat the oven to 200C (400F)
2. Clean beetroot with a brush and plenty of water with a few drops of white vinegar, pat dry and cut into square bite-size pieces
3. Place beetroot into a bowl and mix with ½ teaspoon salt, 1 Tablespoon of olive oil, and freshly ground pepper
4. Line a baking tray (sheet pan), with parchment (baking) paper. Place the beetroot and bake for a total of 30 minutes, checking halfway
5. Peel and cut sweet potato as per beetroot
6. Place sweet potato into the bowl and mix with salt, olive oil, and pepper
7. Bake sweet potato for 15 to 20 minutes. Put in the oven after the beetroot has baked for 15 minutes, at halfway
8. Take roasted vegetables out of the oven. Check if the sweet potato needs extra baking and put back in the oven for 5 more minutes
9. Place fully baked beetroot and sweet potato on a flat cold tray to cool down
10. Wash and dry the lettuce
11. Now we're going to assemble the salad. Choose your favourite serving bowl and place the lettuce. Scatter vegetables over the lettuce and sprinkle with the seeds
12. Serve with the Aceto dressing

Substitute sweet potato with pumpkin. You can also use golden beets, although I love the vibrant colours of this scrumptious salad. Vegetables can be baked in advance. This salad is perfect for picnics and outdoor meals.

Add feta cheese for extra acidity. For a wholesome lunch, add some tuna or soft-boiled eggs.

CHILLI & GARLIC SAUTE GREEN BEANS WITH CHERRY TOMATOES

INGREDIENTS

MAKES 4 TO 6 SERVINGS

- ½ kg (1.1 lb) green beans
- 12 cherry tomatoes
- 1 large garlic clove or 2 medium
- 1 fresh chilli or ¼ teaspoon chilli flakes (crushed red pepper)
- 1 Tablespoon olive oil
- ¼ cup (60ml / 2 oz) white wine
- 1 pinch of saffron threads
- ½ teaspoon salt
- Freshly ground black pepper

I remember watching a cooking show with my husband Cristian, we weren't married yet, where they made a similar dish to this. Of course, I went to the kitchen and created my own version! Over the years I have cooked it plenty of times until I developed the recipe that I share with you here. My relationship with my husband is all around food and travel, as I imagine you have deduced by now. After all, isn't it said "the way to a man's heart is through his stomach"?

1. Wash beans and tomatoes in a bowl with water and a dash of white vinegar
2. Drain vegetables and trim the beans
3. Cut cherry tomatoes in half from top to bottom
4. Heat a heavy bottom pan over medium heat and add the olive oil
5. Smash garlic, peel and fry until golden and reserve (make sure you don't overcook it)
6. Sauté the cherry tomatoes with the chilli and saffron until the tomatoes blister, about 2 to 3 minutes
7. Add trimmed whole green beans, garlic, salt, and pepper and mix all ingredients
8. Pour the wine, shake the pan and cover with a lid
9. Reduce heat to medium-low and cook for 20 to 25 minutes, depending on how crunchy you like your beans
10. Shake the pan a couple of times during cooking
11. Add extra liquid if needed

Serve with *ASADO* (Page 175) or *BAKED TROUT WITH SERRANO HAM* (Page 160).

ROASTED ASPARAGUS

Asparagus is one of my favourite vegetables. I only cook them when they're in season, but I eat plenty of them to last me until the next spring! Roasting is my preferred way to cook them. They're still crunchy and have that lovely roasted flavour. I have developed this recipe in the last couple of years in my kitchen in Northern California. My husband and I love this side dish and cook it frequently.

1. Trim asparagus by bending them close to the bottom end until they naturally break. Discard the hard part
2. Wash and pat dry with a tea towel
3. Preheat the oven to 200C (400F)
4. Prepare a baking tray (sheet pan) with baking (parchment) paper
5. Place asparagus on the tray and drizzle the olive oil, season with salt and pepper and mix well using your hands or tongs
6. Bake for 5 minutes
7. Open the oven door and shake the pan a few times (don't forget using oven mitts), this will roast the asparagus more evenly
8. Bake for 5 more minutes
9. Serve inmediately

This recipe uses green asparagus, but try using white or purple, they're equally delicious.

INGREDIENTS
MAKES 2 TO 4 SERVINGS

- 1 bunch fresh asparagus
- 1 Tablespoon olive oil
- ¼ teaspoon salt
- Freshly ground black pepper

ROASTED BRUSSELS SPROUTS WITH PAPRIKA

Brussels sprouts are one of my most liked vegetables. I have always eaten them, but I'm aware that they're not everybody's 'cup of tea'. I developed this recipe during my time living in the Silicon Valley. My husband and I love roasted vegetables and these Brussels sprouts, with the smokiness of the paprika, are scrumptious. If you like spicy food, bake them using hot paprika. You should be able to find it in specialised Spanish suppliers. You can also add chilli flakes. My favourite parts of this dish are the chips that result from the small loose leaves. Keep an eye on them and take them out of the oven as soon as they turn brown. I think I can eat a whole bowl of them. I may have invented a new superfood!?

INGREDIENTS
MAKES 2 TO 4 SERVINGS

- ½ kg (1.1 lb) Brussels sprouts
- 2 Tablespoons olive oil
- 1 teaspoon smoked Spanish paprika (or hot if you like spicy food)
- ½ teaspoon salt
- Freshly ground black pepper

1. Wash Brussels sprouts in a bowl of water with a dash of white vinegar. Rinse and pat dry with a tea towel
2. Trim the end of the Brussels sprouts and cut in half from top to bottom
3. Don't discard the loose leaves, they will make delicious Brussels sprouts chips
4. Place Brussels sprouts in a bowl and drizzle with olive oil, add paprika, salt and pepper and mix until well coated
5. Cut a piece of baking (parchment) paper to the same size as you baking tray (sheet pan)
6. Preheat the oven to 200C (400F) and place the sheet pan baking tray (sheet pan) to preheat
7. Using oven mitts, carefully place baking (parchment) paper over the baking tray (sheet pan), add Brussels sprouts and bake for 10 minutes
8. Take out the loose leaves when they look brown and crunchy
9. Flip the Brussels sprouts halves and bake for 10 more minutes
10. Serve while warm and enjoy!

This side dish has lots of flavour; it is better served with simple food, such as *ARGENTINIAN ASADO* (Page 175), *BAKED TROUT* (Page 160) or *BUTTERFLY CHICKEN* (Page 172).

Salads & Vegetable Side Dishes

RUSTIC ITALIAN STYLE POTATO SALAD

INGREDIENTS
MAKES 4 SERVINGS

- 500gr (1.1 lb) small potatoes
- ¼ cup chopped fresh parsley
- 2 Tablespoons olive oil
- Salt and pepper to taste

M y daughter started to walk when I learned to make this salad. You can imagine what a warm memory it has for me. We were invited to spend a weekend on Sorrento beach, in the Mornington Peninsula in Australia. I remember the Australian Open was on TV when my friends started screaming as my daughter took her first steps! She got such a fright, but we calmed her down by clapping and telling her she did well. Oh! They grow so fast! I hope when my friends read this they remember what a wonderful time we had that weekend.

1. Bring a pot of salted water to boil
2. Cut potatoes in half with the skin on (leave whole if they are very small)
3. Boil potatoes for 10 minutes or until just tender
4. Strain the potatoes and while hot, drizzle the olive oil, add parsley, and season to taste
5. Mix well and serve warm Buon Appettito!

Soups

"Soup is a lot like a family. Each ingredient enhances the others; each batch has its own characteristics; and it needs time to simmer to reach full flavour."

MARGE KENNEDY

Soups

ASPARAGUS GAZPACHO

I came up with this recipe when I invited a group of ladies for high tea. My dear friend Mary Parfrey had just discovered that she was gluten intolerant. I wanted her to enjoy the food without compromising my style of cooking. I presented this gazpacho as a trio of small shot glasses with red, white, and green gazpacho, which looked amazing! Mary used to be my boss and then she became one of my best friends. She is one of the nicest and most generous people I know. She was at my daughters' birth and that will keep us connected for life.

1. Put a pot with water to boil and add a pinch of salt
2. Trim asparagus by bending them close to the bottom end until they naturally break, discard the hard part
3. Cook asparagus in the boiling water until tender, about 3 minutes
4. Strain asparagus, set aside, and reserve the cooking water
5. Put salt, garlic, and peppercorns in a mortar and pestle and pound until it forms a smooth paste
6. Place almonds in a food processor and mill until just ground
7. Add asparagus, garlic paste, cumin, 2 boiled eggs, olive oil, and vinegar to the food processor and blend until a paste is formed
8. Slowly add the asparagus cooking water until your desired consistency is achieved
9. I like a thick gazpacho when I serve it in a bowl, but for a small gazpacho shot glass, you want a lighter more drinkable consistency. In this case, add more asparagus cooking water. Play with it and have fun!
10. Check the seasoning and adjust it to your preferred taste
11. To garnish chop some hard-boiled eggs and/or jamon (ham) SERRANO CRUMBLES (*)

When asparagus are not in season, replace the fresh asparagus with 2 jars of store bought asparagus and their water. If you have a *NUT ALLERGY*, substitute the almonds for fresh cucumber. This will give you a lighter and fresher gazpacho. You will need less asparagus cooking water to achieve your desired consistency.

Experiment and enjoy it!

INGREDIENTS
MAKES 4 TO 6 SERVINGS

- 500gr (1.1 lb) asparagus
- 1 cup (200gr / 7 oz) almonds
- 2 garlic cloves
- 4 Tablespoons olive oil
- 3 Tablespoons apple cider vinegar, or to taste
- ½ teaspoon Salt
- 4 peppercorns
- 1 teaspoon ground cumin
- 3 hard-boiled eggs
- 3 cups asparagus cooking water

(*) To make the SERRANO CRUMBLES, lay thin slices of *jamón* or prosciutto on a baking sheet (tray) covered with parchment (baking) paper and bake for 10 minutes in a preheated oven to 200C (400F). Place on a cooling rack and crumble with your hands. You can also make it into a powder using a food processor.

FISH SOUP WITH VERMICELLI NOODLES

INGREDIENTS

MAKES 4 TO 6 SERVINGS

- 1kg (2.2 lbs) white fish fillets
- 3 medium carrots cut into cubes
- 3 medium potatoes peeled and cut into cubes
- 3 garlic cloves, smashed and thinly sliced
- 6 scallions (spring/green onions), sliced, including green part
- 1 handful fresh parsley, roughly chopped
- 1 lemon
- 1 Tablespoon olive oil
- 1 teaspoon salt
- Freshly ground pepper to taste
- 250gr (approximately ½ lb) dry rice vermicelli noodles
- 8 cups (2 litres / 64 oz) of water

This is a *GLUTEN-FREE* recipe. If I have to think of someone when I make this soup, it is my dear friend Michele Senanayake. She doesn't eat chicken, so when she got very ill, I had to think of a soup to substitute for my *'cure everything chicken soup'*. Then I remembered my fish soup with noodles. I cooked it with lots of love and delivered it to her house with an explanation of adding vermicelli noodles when they were going to eat it. She got better and her family loved the soup so much, that they added it to their regular menu. I grew up eating this dish on a regular basis. It was one of the first meals I cooked for my husband and I remember him telling his dad how delicious it was.

1. Start by cutting the fish into bite-size pieces and place in the pot of your choice for cooking the soup
2. Add the carrots and potato cubes, garlic, scallions (spring/green onions), and parsley, in this order
3. Juice the lemon and add to the pot together with the olive oil, salt and pepper
4. Gently mix to blend all ingredients, being careful not to break the fish
5. Fill the pot with the water and bring to a gentle boil over medium heat
6. Cover and simmer for 15 minutes. This is a light and fresh soup. We don't want to overcook the fish
7. Add dry noodles to the pot and cook for 5 minutes, or follow the packet instructions
8. Take the soup off the heat, check for seasoning, and serve in bowls with *SPELT FLATBREAD* (page 181)

This soup can be eaten without the noodles for a *LOW CARB* and *PALEO* alternative. Vermicelli noodles can be substituted for any pasta of your choice.

Make it more kid-friendly by adding letters or animal-shaped pasta. For the picky eaters, you can use vegetable-based pasta, they will love it!

Soups

PEA & HAM SOUP

INGREDIENTS
MAKES 6 SERVINGS

- 250gr (0.55 lb / 8.8 oz) frozen peas (use fresh when in season)
- 250gr (0.55 lb / 8.8 oz) green split peas (or green lentils)
- 1 brown onion
- 1 garlic clove
- 3 carrots
- 3 celery sticks
- 1 ham hock or 500gr (1.1 lb) piece of ham
- 1 Tablespoon olive oil
- 1 teaspoon dry thyme (or 1 Tablespoon fresh)
- 1 teaspoon dry parsley (or 1 Tablespoon fresh)
- ½ teaspoon dry rosemary (or 2 teaspoons fresh)
- 8 cups (2 litres / 64 oz) water
- 6 black peppercorns
- 1 teaspoon salt

I was introduced to this hearty and comforting soup during my years working at the CBD (Central Business District) in Melbourne, Australia. It was the perfect lunch to warm me up during the long and cold winters. I love the smoky flavour of the ham and the vibrant green colour of this soup. I really like peas too, so it makes it a winner for me! This recipe is very special for me as I developed it for my daughter, who doesn't like peas. It used to be her childhood favourite soup. She used to get very excited when I put it in her school lunch box. Ah, those days…

1. Place the split peas (or green lentils) in a large bowl, cover with cold water and soak overnight (at least for 5 to 6 hours)
2. Roughly chop the onion, garlic, carrots, and celery
3. Heat the oil in a large pot over medium heat. Stir in the vegetables and cook for 10 minutes
4. Add herbs, one at a time, and stir until fragrant, for 1 to 2 minutes
5. Drain the split peas (or green lentils) and add to the pot together with the peas. Mix with the vegetables and herbs until well combined
6. Add ham hock (or ham) and the water
7. Bring to the boil
8. Cover and simmer for 1.5 to 2 hours. The longer you cook the soup, the stronger the flavours will develop, and the more tender the meat will be
9. Take the pan off the heat
10. Use tongs to remove the ham hock (or ham) from the pot and set aside until it is cool enough to handle
11. Blend the soup to your desire consistency. I like it with a bit of texture, but some people prefer it very creamy
12. With your hands, pull the ham off the bone. Discard the bone and shred the ham
13. Return the ham to the soup, stir and check for seasoning

Serve it with *EASY SPELT FLATBREAD* (Page 181). Yum!

This soup is perfect to cook in a *PRESSURE COOKER* or *INSTANT POT* on the high setting. When you reach to boiling point, simmer for 35 to 45 minutes with a quick pressure release at the end. If you are a *SLOWCOOKER* user, cook for 6 to 8 hours.

Soups

MY CURE EVERYTHING CHICKEN SOUP

Nothing warms your soul like a good bowl of freshly home made chicken soup. The smell already makes you feel better, doesn't it? I cook this soup whenever someone is unwell around me. Everybody feels better shortly after. My family loves it. We eat it regularly during the cold weather. There is a person that always comes to my mind when I cook this soup, Zara. She went to my daughter's school for one year and they became good friends. On a play date after school, I made chicken soup for dinner and served them a bowl with noodles. Zara said it was the best chicken soup she had ever tasted!

1. Rinse and clean the chicken, place in a deep casserole or pot, cover with water and bring to a boil over high-heat. Turn heat to medium and skim the foam from the surface with a metal spoon. (This will take about 15 minutes)

2. Meanwhile, cut the onion in 4 wedges and slice thinly from bottom to top, smash and thinly slice garlic cloves

3. Clean vegetables thoroughly. Cut celery into thin slices and peel the carrots, cut in half lengthways and slice

4. Make a small parcel with a piece of cheesecloth with the dry herbs, bay leaf, and peppercorns. (You don't want to bite into a whole peppercorn!)

5. When there is no more foam, add all vegetables, herb parcel, and salt to the pot. Cover and simmer for 1.5 to 2 hours

6. Place chicken onto a platter. You have to be very careful as the chicken will be very tender and will break easily. Use a pair of tongs to help you. Let the chicken cool down for 15 minutes before you handle it

7. Throw away the herbs parcel, it has done its job infusing the soup

8. Remove the skin of the chicken and shred the meat. I like using my hands to do this. but you can use forks or any other utensil that makes it easier. Give the job to the children, they love doing this!

9. Return chicken meat to the soup and mix well

10. Serve in bowls with a slice of *PANE DI CASA* (Page 186)

This is a really hearty meal. You won't need to add a salad or even dessert.

INGREDIENTS
MAKES 6 SERVINGS

- 1 whole organic free-range chicken
- 1 large brown onion
- 3 garlic cloves
- 3 celery sticks
- 2 large carrots (or 3 medium)
- 12 whole black peppercorns
- 1 dry bay leaf
- ½ teaspoon dry parsley
- ½ teaspoon dry thyme
- 1 teaspoon salt
- 8 cups (2 litres / 64 oz) of water

This recipe is perfect to cook in a PRESSURE COOKER or INSTANT POT. I always make it with my pressure cooker. Once you have finished skimming, add the vegetables and herbs parcel, close the lid and cook on the high setting for 30 minutes. Use the quick steam release option and wait 5 minutes before opening the lid, then continue as indicated above.

Soups

COCIDO

This emblematic and rustic Spanish meal finds its origin in a meal called '*Adafina*', the classic Sephardic Sabbath stew. This dish was traditionally made with lamb. When Spain became Christian and started making use of its main resources, pork was introduced into this soup. The potato came after, with the discovery of the Americas. From its origins to this recipe, there are many cooking hours, three countries, my own upbringing, and two special women. The first one, Maria, from my group of Spanish mums in Melbourne, Australia. She was very sick once and we all got together to feed her in turns. I offered to make cocido as I knew that just by eating the broth she would get better. The second one, Aurora, whom I call my sunshine from Andalucía in California, asked me for help to buy the ingredients to make this soup. It is incredible what strong relationships you create when you live overseas. These people become your family and a very important part of your life.

COCIDO (continued)

1. Prepare a heavy bottom pot
2. Drain the chickpeas (garbanzo beans) and add to the pot
3. Wash and pat dry all the meat
4. Add water to the pot and place the meats inside
5. Put the pot on high heat and bring to the boil
6. When it starts to foam, reduce heat to medium and skim constantly, for about 20 minutes. (Alternatively, you can discard the water at this point. Rinse garbanzos and meats and add clean water. This will give you a clearer stock, but you will miss out on the bone broth goodness and flavour)
7. Cover the pot and simmer for 1 ½ hours, skimming occasionally
8. Add vegetables and simmer for 20 more minutes. You can add 1 to 2 cups of water if the broth (stock) has reduced
9. Let the soup rest for 10 to 15 minutes and check for seasoning before serving

To serve, prepare a tray or platter and place all vegetables and meats, being careful as they will be very tender and may break. Put this serving dish in the middle of the table. Serve the soup with chickpeas (garbanzo beans) in separate individual bowls. Each person will then pick a few of their favourite meats and vegetables for their bowl. This way everybody will eat the complete meal at once.

This recipe is perfect for *PRESSURE COOKING* and *INSTANT POT*. I always make it using my pressure cooker. To do so, after you have finished skimming, add the vegetables, close the lid and cook on the high setting for 30 minutes. Use the quick steam release option and wait 5 minutes before opening the lid. Let the soup rest for 10 to 15 minutes before serving.

You can substitute ossobuco (beef shin) for beef ribs.

When it comes to buying the Serrano ham or prosciutto, I usually ask for the end bit of the whole piece. In many places, they will be happy to sell it for a cheaper price than if you buy the thicker slice.

INGREDIENTS
MAKES 4 TO 6 SERVINGS

- 250gr (0.55 lb / 8.8 oz / 1 ½ cups) dry chickpeas (garbanzo beans), soaked overnight
- 1 whole chicken leg (Maryland), without skin
- 1 piece of ossobuco (beef shin)
- 1 x 1cm (½") thick slice of pork belly
- 1 x 1cm (½") thick slice of Serrano ham or prosciutto
- 1 medium to large leek, cut in half lengthways, white part only
- 2 medium carrots, peeled and cut in half
- 2 large celery sticks without leaves, cut in half
- 2 medium potatoes, peeled
- 1 teaspoon salt
- 8 cups (2 litres / 64 oz) water

PUCHERO CHICO (ARGENTINIAN STYLE SOUP)

Puchero chico is a traditional recipe from Argentina made from leftover *asado*. The flavour of the charcoals in the barbecued meat makes this soup very comforting and tasty. I started making it after I saw my husband cooking it from scratch a few times. I cooked it for my in-laws when they visited us in California. I wanted to have a hearty meal waiting for us after we visited San Francisco for the day. To my surprise, my in-laws really liked it and took notes to cook it at their home. We love this meal and it is a staple at our dinner table during the winter months.

1. Cut meat into bite-size pieces and reserve with all bones (these give extra flavour to the soup)
2. Heat a heavy bottom pot over medium heat and add the oil
3. Sauté onion, celery, carrot, and garlic, stirring occasionally for 5 minutes
4. Add oregano and cumin, one at a time, and mix well
5. Add meat and bones and combine with vegetables and spices
6. Add the rest of the ingredients: lentils, pumpkin (or sweet potato), greens, leftover vegetables, and bay leaf
7. Pour water and season with salt and pepper
8. Bring to the boil, cover and simmer for 1 hour
9. Check for seasoning
10. Let rest for 10 to 15 minutes

Serve with *PANNE DI CASA* (Page 186) and drizzle with chilli oil to add extra spice, or simply with extra virgin olive oil.

If you don't have leftover asado or BBQ meat, seal and brown the ribs before you start making the soup. Then continue as per the recipe.

This soup can be cooked in a *PRESSURE COOKER* or *INSTANT POT* on a high setting for 30 minutes, always with a quick steam release.

This is a *GLUTEN-FREE* recipe.

INGREDIENTS
MAKES 4 TO 6 SERVINGS

- 1kg (2.2 lb) leftover asado, any barbecue meat or beef short ribs
- 100gr (¼ lb) green lentils soaked overnight and strained
- 1 medium **onion**, and 2 cloves **garlic**, finely chopped
- 2 cups (250gr / ½ lb) cubed pumpkin or sweet potato
- 1 celery stick, thinly sliced
- 1 medium carrot peeled and cubed
- 2 good handfuls or 2 cups packed with chopped greens (spinach, chard or kale, or a mix of them)
- 1 cup of any leftover vegetables (broccoli and/or cauliflower stems), cut into cubes
- 1 teaspoon each dry **oregano** and ground **cumin**
- 1 bay leaf
- 6 cups (1.5 litres / 48 oz) water
- 1 Tablespoon **olive oil** and 1 teaspoon **salt**
- Black pepper to taste

— *Soups* —

CAULIFLOWER & KALE SOUP

INGREDIENTS

MAKES 6 SERVINGS

- 1 whole cauliflower (green outer leaves and stem included)
- 1 bunch kale (I use Tuscan)
- 1 medium brown onion
- 2 cloves garlic
- 2 medium potatoes
- 4 cups (1 litre / 32 oz) VEGETABLE STOCK (BROTH; Page 27)
- Water
- 1 teaspoon salt
- 6 black peppercorns
- 1 Tablespoon olive oil plus extra for garnish

I owe this recipe to my husband's cousin, Paula. It was her mum Nene (although her real name is Cristina) who passed it onto me. When I was asked to cater for a conference at our school in Melbourne, I chose this soup as a *PLANT-BASED* option, and also as a soul warming for the cold weather. The response was excellent, and I got a few requests for the recipe. I know it is a bit late, but here it is: *Paula's Cauliflower and Kale Soup* with my touch.

1. Chop onion and garlic
2. Roughly cut cauliflower, kale, and potatoes (previously peeled)
3. Place your favourite pot for cooking soup over medium heat
4. Add olive oil, when warm, fry onion for 3 minutes, stirring occasionally
5. Sauté garlic with onion for 2 extra minutes, until fragrant
6. Add vegetables to the pot and toss until well combined
7. Pour vegetable stock (broth) to cover the vegetables. If needed, add a bit of water, but remember that vegetables release their own liquid
8. Add salt and pepper
9. Cover and simmer over low-to-medium heat for 20 to 30 minutes, depending on how you prefer your vegetables
10. Take off the heat and blend until smooth or your desired consistency
11. If it is too thick, add a bit of extra water
12. Check for seasoning

Serve in bowls and garnish with a drizzle of olive oil, or any flavoured oil of your choice. I like adding chilli oil for a spicy kick, but you can also sprinkle chilli flakes or sliced fresh chillies.

Blue cheese goes well with this soup, and it will give a deeper flavour.

Pair it with a glass of nice white wine and *FLATBREAD* (Page 181).

Make it ahead; it tastes better the next day. This recipe works well using the *INSTANT POT*, *CROCKPOT*, or *SLOW COOKER*. Just follow the instructions for this type of recipe on the manufacturer's manual.

SPRING VEGETABLES MINESTRONE WITH PESTO

INGREDIENTS
MAKES 6 SERVINGS

- 1 medium red onion
- 2 cloves garlic
- 2 medium carrots
- 2 celery sticks without leaves
- 1 bunch asparagus
- 1 cup peas (can be frozen)
- 1 cup fava (broad) beans (can be frozen)
- ½ bunch of kale (or any spring greens of your choice)
- 1 x 400gr (11 oz) tin (can) chopped tomatoes
- 5 cups (1.25 litres / 40 oz) *VEGETABLE STOCK (BROTH; PAGE 27)*
- Olive oil
- 1 teaspoon salt
- Freshly ground black pepper
- 6 Tablespoons *PESTO (Page 40)*

Minestrone is a thick soup of Italian origin made with vegetables, often with the addition of beans and pasta. There is no set recipe for minestrone. I usually make it as a way to use any leftover vegetables in my fridge before they go to waste. Because of its unique origins and the absence of a fixed recipe, minestrone varies widely across Italy depending on traditional cooking times, ingredients, and seasons. I created this recipe for a spring-inspired cooking class. The freshness of the spring vegetables and fava (broad) beans makes a lighter and more appealing soup for warmer weather. The addition of pesto gives it a depth of flavour worth to make a fresh batch if you don't have any in the fridge.

1. Peel and chop onion and carrots
2. Place a heavy bottom pot over medium heat
3. Add 1 Tablespoon olive oil
4. Cut celery in half from the top and then slice
5. Sauté onion, carrots, and celery for 3 minutes, stirring occasionally
6. Crush, peel, and chop garlic
7. Add garlic to vegetables and cook for 2 minutes mixing well
8. Trim asparagus by bending them close to the bottom end until they naturally break. Discard the hard part and break them in bite-size pieces
9. Peel fava (broad) beans, if they're fresh
10. Pour stock (broth) and tomatoes into the pot
11. If fava (broad) beans are fresh, add them now
12. Bring to a boil
13. Reduce heat to low and simmer for 15 minutes
14. Add asparagus, peas, and fava (broad) beans (if these are frozen)
15. Season with salt and pepper
16. Peel and thinly slice kale (or spring greens) and add to the pot
17. Simmer for an extra 15 minutes (this will keep the vegetables nice and fresh)
18. Let the soup rest for 10 to 15 minutes and check for seasoning before serving
19. Add more water or broth (stock) if the soup is too thick
20. Serve in bowls with 1 Tablespoon of *PESTO* (Page 40) and a drizzle of any oil of your choice. I like adding chilli or spicy oil
21. Don't forget the bread! Any recipe from this book will do the trick

Soups

LENTILS & CHORIZO SOUP

Most Spaniards from my generation have grown up eating this type of soup on a regular basis. I have always loved lentils and remember how my sister Rosa and I got excited when we had it for lunch when we were kids. In fact, because of her, I use the combination of red and green capsicum (bell pepper). This version is the way I like eating it. To my surprise, whenever someone has eaten this soup at home, in all places that I have lived, they have always asked me for the recipe. I think it is the flavour of the chorizo when it releases the fat and smoked paprika that gives it that '*umami*' and deliciousness. We owe the touch of cumin to Doña Encarna. I tried her lentils soup when I stayed with my dearest friend Ana, her daughter, on one of my trips to Spain. I quickly identified the cumin and thought it gave it a really nice flavour. She uses turkey chorizo as a substitute for pork.

This soup cooks very well in a *PRESSURE COOKER* and also in the *INSTANT POT*. If you prefer to use a more traditional method, select your favourite pot for cooking soups.

1. Strain the lentils and place them in the pot
2. Slice the chorizo sideways, or to your liking, and add to the pot
3. Add all remaining ingredients, except the water
4. Mix until well combined
5. Add water and place on a medium-to-high heat
6. Bring to the boil, lower heat to medium-low, and simmer for 30 to 45 minutes, depending on how tender the lentils are
7. Let rest for 10 to 15 minutes before serving and check for seasoning

If you decide to use a *PRESSURE COOKER* or *INSTANT POT*, cook for 15 minutes on high setting and release the pressure quickly. Open the pot once all the steam is gone and let stand for 5 minutes before serving.

For a *VEGETARIAN & PLANT-BASED* version, substitute the chorizo for 1 teaspoon of smoked Spanish paprika and use vegetable stock (broth) instead of water. You will love the flavour!

INGREDIENTS
MAKES 4 TO 6 SERVINGS

- 250gr (0.55lb / 1+ ¼ cup) dry green lentils, soaked overnight
- 1 chorizo sausage
- 1 Tablespoon *GARLIC & PARSLEY BLEND* (Page 32)
- 1 large garlic clove, smashed and thinly sliced
- 1 medium brown onion, chopped
- ½ medium **green capsicum** (green bell pepper), and ½ medium **red capsicum** (red bell pepper), cubed
- 1 large ripe **tomato**, 1 large **carrot**, and 1 large **celery** stick, cubed
- 1 large **potato**, peeled and cubed
- ½ bunch of green chard or spinach, thinly sliced
- 1 teaspoon each ground **cumin** & **salt**
- Freshly ground black pepper to taste
- 1 pinch of saffron threads
- 1 dry bay leaf
- 1 Tablespoon olive oil
- 6 cups (1.5 litres/ 48 oz) of water

DAHL

I started using red split lentils when cooking for my little one. These lentils don't need to soak overnight and are much quicker to cook and also easier to digest. *Dahl* is an Indian lentil soup with many versions and variations. I like this simple recipe, as it is very easy to make and always helps me to clean my fridge of leftover vegetables. It is my go-to recipe for no meat days. My *Dahl* was a favourite at the school canteen, especially during the winter months. I remember the first time I made it. I wasn't sure if it was going to work, as I had never cooked it for such a large crowd! But it did work, and it became a regular on our winter menu. My group of volunteers and I were so happy to feed the children such healthy and soul warming food.

1. Heat oil in a large heavy-based pot
2. Cook onion, garlic, and ginger, stirring until the onion is translucent, for about 2 minutes
3. Add carrot and celery and sauté for 3 more minutes
4. Incorporate spices, one at a time, stirring constantly
5. Add lentils, tomatoes, spinach, and stock (broth) and mix well
6. Season with salt and pepper
7. Reduce heat, cover and simmer for 1 hour
8. Check halfway and add more liquid if it looks dry
9. Just before serving, check for seasoning and add the coriander (cilantro)
10. Add chilli oil or chilli flakes to make it spicy
11. You can also add coconut milk or cream for a different texture and flavour

Serve with *PERFECT WHITE RICE* (Page 138), *PARATHA* (Page 194), and *CUCUMBER & FRESH MINT SALAD* (Page 95), as shown on the image on pages 164 & 165. Experiment with different types of lentils, or even a mix of them. You will get different textures and flavours. You may create your own recipe that you and your loved ones will love.

This recipe is perfect for *PRESSURE COOKING* and *INSTANT POT*. In fact, I always make it using my beloved pressure cooker. In both cases, cook on the high setting for 15 minutes. Use the quick release steam option and wait 5 extra minutes before you open the pot.

INGREDIENTS
MAKES 4 TO 6 SERVINGS

- 300gr (0.66 lb / 10.58 oz / 1 ½ cups) red split lentils soaked for about 2 hours
- 1 Tablespoon olive oil
- 1 medium red onion, finely chopped
- 1 garlic, finely chopped
- 1 teaspoon grated fresh ginger (or paste)
- 1 medium carrot, peeled and chopped
- 2 medium celery sticks, chopped
- 2 handfuls fresh spinach leaves, chopped (or any green leaves in your fridge)
- 1 teaspoon each ground **coriander, cumin & turmeric**
- 1 pinch saffron threads
- 1 x 400gr (11oz) tin (can) chopped tomatoes
- 2 cups *VEGETABLE STOCK (BROTH*; Page 27)
- 1 good handful coarsely chopped fresh coriander (cilantro)
- Salt & pepper to taste

SPINACH & TOFU SOUP

INGREDIENTS
MAKES 4 SERVINGS

- 6 cups (1.5 litres / 48 oz) *VEGETABLE STOCK (BROTH;* Page 27)
- 1 x 454gr (1 lb/ 16 oz) block organic silken tofu
- 4 handfuls of fresh spinach leaves
- Tamari sauce (or soy)
- Sesame oil

The same "*you should never judge a book by its cover*", goes for eating places. I ate this soup at a small Chinese eatery in Northern California. We were looking for the best dumplings in the Bay Area and this place was recommended as the top one. When we arrived at the small shopping strip and saw the small restaurant, we were a bit suspicious. However, it was full of people and that gave us the confidence that the food would be good and authentic. We weren't wrong. The food was simple but truly authentic and delicious. This soup came as a surprise. Served with chicken broth, it was light and fresh but very comforting. I pointed out that it should be *PLANT-BASED*, and that's what I have done with this recipe.

1. Heat the broth (stock) in a deep casserole over medium heat
2. Cut tofu into dice size cubes
3. Wash spinach leaves thoroughly
4. Add tofu and spinach to the broth and cook for 5 minutes
5. Serve the soup in medium bowls
6. Season with 1 teaspoon of Tamari sauce and a few drops of sesame oil for each bowl

I like serving this soup for lunch or as part of a Chinese banquet. It is a great supper too. It takes less than 15 minutes to cook if you have the broth (stock) already made. I am sure you will make it regularly.

Pasta & Rice

"Life is a combination of magic and pasta"

FEDERICO FELLINI

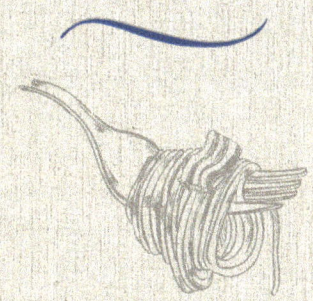

— Pasta & Rice —

BASIC SPELT PASTA RECIPE

My husband started making fresh pasta at home, but once I got more serious about being a *'foodie'* I started making it myself and experimenting using different flours. I started using spelt flour when making *PIZZA* (Page 189) and I quickly discovered that spelt pasta is easier to digest and higher in fibre than wheat. My fondest memory of making pasta is the time that Juan, my niece Mayte's partner, and I teamed up to make his glorious spicy tomato and clams pasta sauce. I made the pasta from scratch and by hand, even the rolling! We had lots of fun and made a mess of the kitchen, but it was worth it as we all truly enjoyed the meal and being together. My niece and her partner are one of the nicest couples I know. Don't think that I'm biased! It's true. I love being with them, and their sweet rabbit Piwi, whenever I visit Spain.

1. Put flours and salt in the bowl of a food processor and pulse a couple of times

BASIC SPELT PASTA RECIPE (continued)

2. Add eggs and olive oil and pulse until they resemble chewy-looking breadcrumbs
3. Keep pulsing until it starts to come together into larger balls of dough
4. Put the dough on your kitchen bench and work by hand for 2 minutes until you get a smooth and elastic dough
5. Wrap the dough in a tea towel and let rest in the fridge for, at least, 30 minutes. (Pasta works better if you make it in advance)
6. Remove the dough from the fridge and divide into 4 balls
7. Start working with one ball while keeping the rest wrapped
8. Flatten the ball slightly with the palm of your hand and run the dough through the thickest setting of your pasta machine
9. Fold this piece in two and pass again. Repeat this process 3 times to work the gluten in the flour
10. Now start passing the dough through thinner settings one at a time, until you have a thin and large layer of lovely fresh pasta!
11. Cut in half and dust with a mix of the two flours to avoid sticking
12. Repeat with remaining balls and then prepare to shape the pasta to your liking (spaghetti, fettuccini...)
13. To cook the pasta, prepare a pot with boiling salted water and cook the pasta until al dente. Fresh pasta needs 2 to 3 minutes to cook. Keep in mind that pasta will keep cooking with the hot sauce, that's why it is best to cook it *'al dente'*.

Fresh pasta can also be rolled by hand with a long rolling pin and cut with a knife or pizza cutter in different shapes. This is the way it used to be done in the past, and it is still done by the *nonnas* (grandmas) in Italy. I find it very enjoyable and therapeutic. Give it a try! and see which way you prefer to roll your pasta.

This recipe works well with plain (all-purpose) flour. Just add 3 whole eggs, oil & salt.

INGREDIENTS
MAKES 4 TO 6 SERVINGS

- 1 cup (150gr / 0.33 lb / 5.29 oz) Spelt flour
- 1 cup (150gr / 0.33 lb / 5.29 oz) Semolina flour
- 3 eggs + 1 egg yolk (put the egg white in the fridge and use it to make STRAWBERRY & BASIL SORBET – Page 216) (If the eggs are large, you may only need 3; check dough consistency before you add the extra yolk)
- 1 Tablespoon olive oil
- Pinch of salt
- Extra flour and semolina for dusting (equal amount of the two)

ZUCCHINI CARBONARA

INGREDIENTS
MAKES 4 TO 6 SERVINGS

- 1 *BASIC SPELT PASTA RECIPE* (Page 128)
- 2 Tablespoons olive oil
- 1 medium zucchini (courgette), peeled and cut into chunks
- 1 garlic clove, smashed and peeled
- 4 to 6 rashers (slices) of bacon cut into small strips (depending on how much you like bacon)
- 2 eggs at room temperature
- 60gr (½ cup) grated Parmesan or Pecorino cheese, plus extra to grate over cooked pasta
- 1 Tablespoon salt
- Salt & pepper to taste

Or as my daughter calls it: *"creamy pasta sauce."* I became aware of the versatility of using zucchini in pasta sauces when cooking at the school canteen. I learned from my first kitchen mentor, Paola Coccis, to make creamy nut-free pesto using zucchini, which the children loved. Using this principle, I created this sauce one night when my daughter requested creamy pasta for dinner. After her feedback: *"Mami, this is the best creamy pasta ever!"* I never looked back at using real cream in my carbonara sauce. And now you can make it too! This is a great way to use less dairy in the sauce and hide extra vegetables for the picky eaters.

1. Prepare a pot with water and add 1 Tablespoon of salt and 1 Tablespoon of olive oil
2. Bring water to a boil and cook the zucchini for 5 minutes, or until it is soft enough to be blended. Set aside to cool down and reserve
3. Heat 1 Tablespoon of oil in a saucepan over medium heat
4. Cook garlic and bacon until golden and fragrant, turn off the heat and set aside
5. Cook fresh pasta in the boiling water for 2 to 3 minutes
6. Blend zucchini, cheese, and raw eggs in a food processor until a sauce is formed
7. Reserve ½ cup of the cooking zucchini and pasta water
8. Drain pasta, return it to the pot, and drizzle with olive oil to avoid sticking
9. Pour sauce, garlic, and bacon over pasta and mix through
10. Add cooking pasta water (starting with ¼ cup), season with salt and pepper and stir until sauce is well combined with the pasta
11. Serve in a bowl or plate with extra grated Parmesan or Pecorino cheese and freshly ground back pepper

Use any dry pasta of your choice if you're short of time to make fresh pasta. You can also cook your favourite *GLUTEN-FREE* pasta. In both cases, follow the instructions in the packet when cooking the pasta.

For a *VEGETARIAN* version, stay away from the bacon, but still, fry the smashed garlic. This gives the sauce a really nice flavour. It is worth the small effort.

LASAGNA WITH SPINACH PASTA

INGREDIENTS
MAKES 4 TO 6 SERVINGS

- 4 to 6 rashers (slices) of bacon
- ½ kg (1.1 lb) minced beef
- ½ kg (1.1 lb) minced turkey or chicken
- 1 medium red onion
- 4 medium garlic cloves (or 2 big)
- 2 medium carrots (or 1 large)
- 1 large celery stick (or 2 medium)
- 1 teaspoon dry oregano
- ¼ cup red wine
- ¼ cup white wine (or ½ cup rosé in total)
- 2 tins (cans) tomato puree (400gr / 14.5 oz each)
- Extra Virgin olive oil
- Salt & pepper to taste
- 2 big fresh buffalo mozzarella balls
- Parmesan or Pecorino cheese

I have to agree with Anthony Bordain[5] that you don't need to boil fresh pasta when making lasagna. This is my daughter's favourite meal by far. I always make an effort to make it for her on special occasions (or whenever she requests it). Working with Italian restaurateurs for many years has allowed me to learn a few things about their traditional and rustic cooking. My Italian also improved a lot! This recipe is my take on the meat lasagna that Federico, my favourite Italian chef, explained to me. My daughter is a huge fan. I have added the spinach lasagna as it goes really well with the red *Ragú* (Bolognese) sauce. It also adds extra vitamins; besides, I always look for ways to add extra greens in my food.

FOR THE SPINACH PASTA:

1. Follow the recipe for the *BASIC SPELT PASTA* (Page 128) substituting 2 eggs for 170gr (6 oz approximately) fresh spinach leaves
2. Blanch the spinach leaves in a pot of boiling salted water and press them through a sieve (or use a potato ricer) to remove most of the water
3. Process the spinach with the egg in a food processor and then add flours as per the pasta recipe

FOR THE RAGÚ:

1. Place a medium heavy bottom pot over medium heat
2. Slice the bacon and cook until golden brown and reserve
3. Cook meat in bacon fat until browned and reserve; you can do this in batches (you may need to increase the heat)
4. Finely chop onion, carrots, and celery; heat 1 Tablespoon of oil
5. Cook onion, carrots, and celery for 5 minutes, stirring regularly
6. Crush, peel and chop garlic cloves
7. Add garlic to the vegetables and sauté for 2 minutes
8. Add dry oregano and stir for 1 minute
9. Pour wines, mix and cook until all liquid has evaporated

---

[5] Appetites a Cookbook

LASAGNA WITH SPINACH PASTA (continued)

10. Return bacon and meat to the pot and stir well
11. Pour tomato puree, mix and season with salt and pepper to taste
12. Bring to the boil, reduce heat to medium-low, cover and cook for ½ hour
13. Check for seasoning and add water or stock (broth) if the sauce looks a bit dry
14. Cook for 30 more minutes; taste the sauce and adjust seasoning if necessary
15. Remove from the heat and allow to cool

TO ASSEMBLE THE LASAGNA:

16. Slice mozzarella and grate the parmesan cheese
17. Spread a thin layer of *Ragù* on a lasagna tray. Mine is 25 by 18cm (9.8" by 7"/ 2.8ltr / 3 Qt approximately)
18. Top with pasta sheets until fully covered
19. Spread another layer of *Ragù* over the pasta
20. Brake mozzarella slices and scatter over the sauce. Fill the gaps with parmesan cheese
21. Continue building the lasagna in layers, finishing with *Ragù* on the top
22. Fully cover the sauce with mozzarella and parmesan
23. Preheat the oven to 200C (400F)
24. Bake lasagna for 30 to 40 minutes, making sure the cheese on the top is melted but not burnt
25. Take the lasagna out of the oven and let it rest for 15 minutes before serving

I know what you're thinking, too much work! Well, I assure you that you will have fun and the flavour of the dish is well worth the extra effort.

If you have leftover pasta, dry it overnight and store it in a glass jar. I do this all the time and I always have spinach pasta (or green pasta, as my daughter still calls it) ready to cook.

The *Ragù* sauce can be made in a *PRESSURE COOKER* or *INSTANT POT*. Once you have taken it to the boil, set the pressure to high and cook for 20 minutes with quick steam release. This is the way I usually make it. I find it cooks quicker, I use less energy and the flavour intensifies. For Instant Pot use the Stew setting or follow the manufacturer instructions.

Lasagna can be made in advance and it also freezes very well. To reheat, bring it to room temperature and place in the oven covered with wet parchment (baking) paper for 15 minutes at 180C (350F).

— Pasta & Rice —

CHICKEN & GREENS RAVIOLI

My husband's auntie made this dish for my daughter when she went to Argentina with her dad for the first time. My husband immediately told me we had another way to give our daughter extra greens. I have recently met Mecha in person. Our connection was immediate. We both knew each other through my husband and his parents, but the love and respect for each other were already there. I always wanted to know how she cooked this recipe. Unfortunately, we didn't have the opportunity to cook it together but at least she explained how she makes it. This recipe is my interpretation, making the pasta and filling my own way. I have substituted her original spinach for leafy greens, as I find you can use any greens that you have in your fridge or a combination of them. I hope she agrees with my way of cooking it and we can make it together soon.

FOR THE PASTA:

1. Follow the recipe for the *BASIC SPELT PASTA* (Page 128) substituting spelt for plain (all-purpose) flour and using 3 eggs only
2. Pass the pasta through the machine at an extra thin setting (1mm approximately) to have a lighter ravioli

CHICKEN & GREENS RAVIOLI (continued)

FOR THE FILLING:

1. Place a medium heavy bottom pan over medium heat
2. Heat 1 Tablespoon of oil
3. Sauté *GARLIC & PARSLEY BLEND* for 1 minute
4. Add minced meat and cook until all liquid has evaporated.
5. Wash the leafy greens, making sure you remove all the sand
6. Finely chop greens and add to the meat
7. Mix well and fry until greens are wilted
8. Season with salt, pepper, and nutmeg
9. Remove from the heat and allow to cool
10. Place meat mixture in a food processor
11. Add ricotta cheese and blend until you have a paste

TO MAKE THE RAVIOLI:

1. Place pasta over a floured bench and cut into squares with a knife or pasta cutter
2. Spoon 1 Tablespoon of filling over half of the pasta squares (be careful not to overfill)
3. Brush the exposed pasta lightly with water and cover with another square of pasta
4. Gently seal around the filling
5. Place ravioli on a tray floured with flour and semolina mixture to avoid sticking
6. You will get around 35 (68mm / 2.67" square) raviolis
7. Fill a large pot with water, add 1 Tablespoon salt and 1 Tablespoon of olive oil
8. Bring to the boil, add raviolis to boiling water and cook for 2 to 3 minutes
9. Strain and mix with *TOMATO PASSATA* (Page 37)

Raviolis freeze well. If you have leftovers, place them on a tray and freeze them overnight. Once frozen, put in a glass container and keep it in the freezer for up to 1 month.

Make any leftover pasta into fettuccini or spaghetti and leave them to dry for later use.

INGREDIENTS

MAKES 4 TO 6 SERVINGS

- ½ kg (1.1 lb) minced (ground) turkey or chicken
- 1 Tablespoon *GARLIC & PARSLEY BLEND* (Page 32)
- 1 bunch of chard (approximately 150gr / 0.33 lb / 5.29 oz)
- Extra Virgin olive oil
- ¼ cup ricotta cheese
- ¼ teaspoon ground nutmeg
- Salt & pepper to taste

— Pasta & Rice —

GNOCCHI

I discovered the secret of the perfect gnocchi from Mary Antico. She is my dear friend Nina's mum (*FETA AND AVOCADO DIP, Page* 68). Another lovely Mary in my life! I love her vibrant and kind personality. She's an excellent cook too! I remember her explaining to me how to make velvety gnocchi; you need to boil the potatoes beforehand and let them cool down. This way, you use the right amount of flour to achieve tender, silky, and light gnocchi. I prefer to steam the potatoes as they don't absorb water. Sadly, Mary and I have never cooked them together, but I always think of her when I make gnocchi.

1. Peel and cut the potatoes into cubes
2. Steam potatoes for 25 to 30 minutes; starting with cold water
3. Allow to cool completely. It is better to cook potatoes in the morning and knead the gnocchi in the afternoon

GNOCCHI (continued)

4. In a large bowl, crush the cooked potatoes until they are broken, but not too ground. I do this with a large fork or a potato masher
5. Sift the flour with the salt; this will help to have lighter gnocchis
6. Add 300-350gr (2 cups) of the flour and salt, oil, and the beaten egg to the potatoes
7. Knead until it forms a homogenous dough, without overworking. This step can be done with a stand or hand mixer at a slow speed, using the hook attachment
8. Sprinkle some flour on the kitchen bench and knead the dough until you get a texture that is not very sticky. Try not to add too much flour
9. Roll the dough into a tube about 2 fingers (1") wide
10. Cut into pieces of about 2cm (1")
11. Shape gnocchis with the back of a fork or with a gnocchi board. You can also skip this step
12. Cook in boiling water with plenty of salt
13. When gnocchis rise to the surface they are cooked
14. Have a bowl ready with olive oil, to prevent from sticking, and remove gnocchi as they rise to the surface of the boiling water

Serve with your favourite sauce. I like to serve them with *PESTO* (Page 40) and simple *TOMATO SAUCE* (Page 37).

Gnocchis can be frozen. Make a big batch and you will have another meal ready in no time, or an easy lunch to prepare in the morning to take to school or work. To freeze, put the gnocchi in a floured tray and separate them. Place the tray in the freezer for 3-4 hours. Once frozen, keep gnocchis in a bag in the freezer and you will always have fresh gnocchis to eat. They can be cooked from frozen.

INGREDIENTS
MAKES 4 TO 6 SERVINGS

- 1kg (2.2 lbs) desiree (red) potatoes (*TIPS & TRICKS*, Page 21)
- 400 - 450gr (0.90 lb./ 14 oz) plain (all-purpose) flour, sifted (about 3 cups)
- 2 teaspoons olive oil plus extra
- 1 egg
- Salt

PERFECT WHITE RICE

INGREDIENTS
MAKES 4 SERVINGS

- 1 Cup *Basmati* rice
- 1 ½ cups *VEGETABLE STOCK* (*BROTH*; Page 27)

I learned to use this method of cooking rice by absorption thanks to Winifred. Originally from the Philippines, I met him in Australia through my dear friend, Raj. They used to work together. I haven't seen him or heard about him for years. I wonder if he even remembers me! But this recipe has stayed with me since the day he gave it to my husband. I remember it was printed on a yellow paper, which after our move to California, I cannot find, like many other recipes. I'm glad it's so easy and it always works. I make it all the time.

1. Place dry rice in a cooking pot and cover with cold water
2. Mix with your hands or using a spatula until the water becomes cloudy
3. Strain and repeat this process 2 more times
4. Return washed and strained rice to the cooking pot and pour stock (broth)
5. Place the cooking pot over high heat and bring to the boil, cover and simmer for 10 minutes
6. When cooked, **DO NOT OPEN THE LID** and let rest for 5 more minutes
7. Uncover and separate the rice with a fork

This rice is very versatile. I like using Basmati rice because I find it easier to digest, but any long grain rice will work with this method of cooking.

Pasta & Rice

SEAFOOD PAELLA

Paella is said to be a perfect union between two cultures from Spain, the Romans, for the pan, and the Arabs that brought the rice. There is an old story of how the Moorish kings' servants created rice dishes by mixing the leftovers from royal banquets in large pots to take home. It is also said that the word *paella* originates from the Arab word '*baqiyah*' meaning leftovers. The term Paella actually refers to the pan that it is cooked in. Paella's modern form originated in the mid-19th century in the area around Albufera lagoon on the east coast of Spain, adjacent to the city of Valencia; thus, the term '*Paella Valenciana*'. This is my favourite paella. It is the one that brings me memories from my childhood and tastes like the Mediterranean Sea.

1. Use the heads and shells of 8 prawns (shrimps) to make the *SEAFOOD FUMET*. Keep the other four whole to decorate the paella
2. Keep clams (pipis) in water with plenty of salt and some white vinegar (this will get rid of any sand). Take out using tongs and rinse under running cold water before using to decorate the paella
3. Heat the paella pan over medium heat
4. Add 1 Tablespoon of olive oil and cook red capsicum (bell pepper) for about 3 to 5 minutes, until soft and brown; set aside
5. Now is the time to make the famous '*sofrito*'. Add more oil (if needed) and reduce the heat to a medium-low so that the garlic and spices don't burn, or it will give your rice a bitter taste
6. Add garlic and *GARLIC & PARSLEY BLEND* and cook for 1 minute. Add spices, one at a time, stirring constantly, making sure they don't burn
7. Add grated tomato and stir through for 2 minutes, until all the liquid dries out
8. Pour wine and cook until the liquid has evaporated
9. At this point stir the rice into the pan until well coated. It should look translucent

INGREDIENTS
MAKES 6 TO 8 SERVINGS

- ½ kg (1.1 lb) fresh calamari chopped into bite-size pieces, tentacles included (if any)
- 12 jumbo prawns (shrimps) in their shells and heads
- 1 good handful mussels, thoroughly cleaned
- 1 good handful clams (pipis)
- 1 red capsicum (bell pepper), cut into thin strips
- 1 large ripe tomato, grated
- 2 Tablespoons *GARLIC & PARSLEY BLEND* (Page 32)
- 2 garlic cloves, smashed and thinly chopped

SEAFOOD PAELLA (continued)

10. Pour the hot *SEAFOOD FUMET*
11. Add calamari and '*naked*' prawns (shrimps)
12. From this point shake the pan, but do not stir. This will ensure the rice will be nice and loose
13. Season with salt and pepper and spread out cooked red bell pepper (capsicum) and peas
14. Decorate the paella by placing the whole 4 prawns (shrimps) with the shells and scattering the mussels and clams (pipis) all over the dish in a nice pattern of your choice
15. Bring paella to the boil; reduce heat to medium and cook for 13 minutes
16. Increase the heat to maximum and cook for 2 extra minutes (you will cook the paella for 15 minutes in total) to make the '*socarrat*' (rice that gets crunchy and forms a crust at the bottom of the pan) that is so characteristic and popular
17. Take paella off the heat and let rest for 5 minutes covered with a clean tea towel. Traditionally, paella is covered with newspapers

Serve with a sprinkle of fresh parsley and a drizzle of fresh lemon.

I'm not a fan of mixing meat with seafood or fish, but you can add some chicken and/or pork to make a '*paella mixta*'. For this, make sure to add some chicken bones or carcass to your *FUMET*.

INGREDIENTS
CONTINUED

- 2 teaspoons smoked paprika
- 2 teaspoons ground cumin
- 1 heaping pinch saffron threads
- ½ cup of white wine
- 2 to 3 Tablespoons olive oil
- 1 cup peas
- 2 cups '*Bomba*' rice (special paella rice from Spain)
- 4 cups (1 litre / 32 oz) of hot *SEAFOOD FUMET* (Page 31); keep it on low heat while cooking
- 1 lemon cut in 6 wedges
- Salt and black pepper to taste
- Fresh parsley for garnish

— Pasta & Rice —

PEROL

INGREDIENTS
MAKES 6 TO 8 SERVINGS

- 2 cups short-grain rice (or 'Bomba' Spanish paella rice)
- 6 cups (1.5 litres / 48 oz) HOT CHICKEN BROTH (STOCK; Page 28)

The name *PEROL* comes from the pot that it is used to cook this dish. It is not only a traditional recipe from my hometown in Spain; it's part of the culture of the city and its province. It is a social event where friends and families gather together in the countryside and cook the dish over a wood fire. I have grown up attending these events all my childhood and keep very fond memories. This is my favourite rice dish. I love its warmth and humble comfort. It's one of my daughter's favourite meal too.

1. Infuse saffron with 1 Tablespoon of boiling water and set aside
2. Add 1 Tablespoon of olive oil to a hot casserole pot (a wok is perfect to cook this dish) and sear the chicken until golden, being careful not to overcook it. This can be done in batches

Municipal File Cordoba, Spain F0010209-D-0002-236

PEROL (continued)

3. Remove the chicken and set aside
4. Add extra oil to the pot, if needed, and cook onion, *GARLIC & PARSLEY BLEND*, garlic, and bell pepper (capsicum) for about 3 to 5 minutes
5. Add grated tomato and stir through for 2 minutes, until all the liquid has evaporated. This is the 'sofrito' and base of the dish
6. Add the spices, one at a time, starting with cumin, stirring constantly to avoid burning the paprika
7. Return chicken to the pot, add the saffron and its water, and mix with vegetables and spices
8. Pour wine in and cook until all liquid is fully evaporated
9. At this point, add the rice and stir until well coated with all ingredients
10. Pour in the hot broth (stock)
11. Add peas
12. Shake the pot a couple of times (do not stir! We're not making risotto), taste and adjust the seasoning
13. Bring to the boil, reduce the heat and simmer for 15 minutes
14. Take off the heat and let it rest for 5 minutes covered with a clean tea towel or an old newspaper (yes! That's the traditional way)
15. Serve with a wedge of lemon

This dish is perfect to make it *PLANT-BASED*, substituting the meat for all types of vegetables of your choice and using vegetable stock (broth). Add asparagus, artichokes, and fava beans in spring; eggplant (aubergine), zucchini, red bell pepper (capsicum), and cauliflower in winter. The combinations are endless, and you will love it!

Que aproveche!

INGREDIENTS CONTINUED

- 750gr (1.5 lb) chicken thigh cut into bite-size pieces
- 1 cup peas (can be frozen)
- 1 large ripe **tomato**, grated and 1 green **cupsicum** (bell pepper), finely chopped
- 1 medium brown onion, finely chopped
- 2 Tablespoons *GARLIC & PARSLEY BLEND* (Page 32)
- 2 cloves garlic smashed and finely chopped
- 1 ½ teaspoons smoked Spanish paprika
- 1 ½ teaspoons ground cumin
- 1 large pinch saffron threads
- ½ cup (125ml / 4 oz) white wine
- Olive oil
- Salt & pepper to taste
- 1 Lemon cut in 6 wedges

Pasta & Rice

BAKED QUAIL PAELLA

Baked paella or rice is a traditional dish from the Levante area in Spain. I owe knowing how to make it to my sister Mayte, who has been living in the area for many years. I developed this recipe after I visited my auntie Leo (Leonor) and I looked at her cooking rice. She told me about using quail. My auntie is a very special person to me; she is my godmother. I hope she is proud of this dish.

1. Preheat the oven to 200C (400F)
2. Butterfly the quails by cutting through the backbone. Press the breast to flatten them and clean with a kitchen paper towel

BAKED QUAIL PAELLA (continued)

3. Heat your favourite oven-safe pot over medium heat. Add 1 Tablespoon of olive oil and sear the quails in batches until brown on both sides. This will take 2 to 3 minutes per side
4. Place cooked quails in a tray, season with salt and pepper, and reserve
5. If needed, add another Tablespoon of oil to the pan and sauté the capsicum (bell pepper) until brown and soft, but not overcooked. Place in a tray and reserve
6. Now is the time to make the 'sofrito'. Add more oil and reduce the heat to a medium-low so that the garlic and spices don't burn, or it will give your rice a bitter taste
7. Add the 2 Tablespoons of GARLIC & PARSLEY BLEND and stir until fragrant, for about 1 minute. Add garlic and grated tomatoes and cook for 1 to 2 minutes. Add spices, one at a time, stirring constantly, making sure they don't burn
8. Pour wine over 'sofrito' and cook until liquid is fully evaporated. You will be left with a red paste. At this point stir the rice into the pan until well coated
9. Now is the time to add the broth (stock). From this point shake the pan, but DO NOT STIR. This will ensure the rice will be nice and loose
10. Season with salt and pepper and scatter cooked red bell pepper (capsicum) and peas. Place quails evenly over the broth and bake the rice for 15 minutes
11. Take out of the oven, cover with newspaper or a tea towel, and let it rest for 5 minutes

To plate, serve 2 scoops of rice on a plate, place one quail cut in the middle over the rice, and a wedge of lemon, for every guest.

Wait to be praised for a wonderful meal!

INGREDIENTS
MAKES 6 TO 8 SERVINGS

- 6 quails
- 1 red capsicum (bell pepper), cut into strips
- 2 Tablespoons GARLIC & PARSLEY BLEND (Page 32)
- 2 garlic cloves, thinly chopped
- 1 large ripe tomato, grated
- 2 teaspoons smoked paprika
- 2 teaspoons ground cumin
- 1 heaping pinch saffron threads
- ½ cup (125ml / 4 oz) white wine
- 2 to 3 Tablespoons olive oil
- 1 cup peas
- 2 cups 'Bomba' rice (special paella rice from Spain)
- 4 cups (1 litre / 32 oz) hot CHICKEN BROTH (STOCK; Page 28)
- 1 lemon cut in 6 wedges
- Salt & black pepper to taste

CHORIZO & FENNEL RISOTTO

INGREDIENTS
MAKES 6 TO 8 SERVINGS

- 2 cups *Arborio* rice
- 1 chorizo sausage, peeled and sliced
- 1 small fennel, white part only, finely chopped (add the green leafy part to the stock / broth for extra flavour)
- 1 small leek, cut in half and thinly sliced (white part only)
- ½ medium brown onion, finely chopped
- 4 cloves garlic, crushed
- ¾ cup (187.5ml / 6 oz) white wine
- 6 cups (1.5 litres / 48 oz) *VEGETABLE* (Page 27) or *CHICKEN STOCK* (*BROTH*; Page 28)
- 1 to 2 Tablespoons olive oil
- 1 teaspoon salt
- Black pepper to taste
- 2 Tablespoons butter
- Parmesan cheese

My husband is the risotto king! It must be his Italian blood. We created this recipe on one of our cycling trips around Victoria in Australia. My daughter and I followed him on his bicycle adventures. We also wanted to have a holiday (vacation) plus we got to cheer him on and share his achievements. We love the fusion of flavours and cultures in this dish. We came up with it by gathering a few ingredients and leftover stock (broth) in our freezer. It is our favourite risotto by far.

1. Heat the stock (broth) and keep warm
2. Place a thick bottom pan over medium heat and add 1 Tablespoon of oil
3. Fry chorizo slices until brown and crispy, turning halfway; about 1 minute each side. Reserve for later
4. Add fennel, leek, onion, garlic, ½ teaspoon salt and cook until soft and tender; approximately 5 minutes. You can add 1 extra Tablespoon of oil if it looks dry
5. Add the rice to the pan and coat well with the vegetable mixture until it becomes translucent, for about 2 minutes
6. Pour wine and stir, allowing the alcohol to evaporate, 2 to 3 minutes in total
7. Prepare a ladle and a wooden spoon (you should always cook using wooden spoons)
8. Pour 4 to 5 ladles of stock (broth) over the rice and start to stir with gentle moves, until all liquid is absorbed
9. Keep adding 1 to 2 ladles at a time and mix well, until you have used all the broth (stock). You want your risotto to be smooth and moist
10. Take the pan off the heat
11. Add butter and chorizo to the rice and gently stir to combine
12. Check for seasoning
13. Cover and let it rest for 5 min

Serve with grated Parmesan cheese and enjoy!

For a *VEGETARIAN* version, use vegetable stock (broth) and substitute the chorizo for 1 teaspoon of smoked Spanish paprika. Fry paprika with the vegetables, making sure it doesn't burn, or it will give a bitter flavour. To make it *PLANT-BASED* and *DAIRY-FREE*, discard the butter at the end and drizzle with extra virgin olive oil. This is a *GLUTEN-FREE* recipe.

Pasta & Rice

TUNA & KALAMATA PILAF

I am a huge recipe collector. This pilaf (or cheat risotto as my husband calls it) came to me in a recipe card collection from a local supermarket. As with any other recipe, I tested it several times until I gave it my own 'style'. I always have tins (cans) of tuna in my pantry and Kalamata olives in the fridge, so this recipe is one that I cook when I'm short of ingredients, or ideas of what to make for dinner. Being *GLUTEN-FREE*, it's a great recipe when I have guests with Gluten intolerance.

Pasta & Rice

TUNA & KALAMATA PILAF (continued)

1. Strain tuna, break into bite-size pieces, and reserve the oil (if any)
2. Peel and chop the onion
3. Place a heavy bottom saucepan over medium heat
4. Add 1 Tablespoon of the tuna reserved oil (or olive oil)
5. Sauté onion for 3 minutes, until it turns translucent
6. Stir in *GARLIC & PARSLEY BLEND* and cook for 2 more minutes
7. Add the rice to the pan and coat well with the oil, for about 2 minutes
8. Pour the wine, stir and cook until all liquid is evaporated (I love this smell!)
9. Add stock (broth), tuna pieces, and Kalamata olives
10. Season with salt & pepper
11. Gently stir to blend all ingredients
12. Bring pilaf to the boil
13. Reduce heat to medium-low, cover and cook for 15 minutes, stirring every 5 minutes
14. Let pilaf rest for 5 minutes before serving

Please, do not add Parmesan cheese! Italians never mix cheese with seafood or fish.

Drizzle with extra virgin olive oil and add some freshly ground salt and pepper for extra flavour.

Serve it with *GREEN SALAD* (Page 94).

INGREDIENTS
MAKES 4 TO 6 SERVINGS

- 1 medium brown onion
- 2 cups *Arborio* rice
- 4 cups (1 litre / 32 oz) *VEGETABLE STOCK* (BROTH; Page 27)
- 400gr (14 oz approximately) tinned (canned) tuna in olive oil (if possible)
- ½ cup pitted Kalamata olives
- 2 Tablespoons *GARLIC & PARSLEY BLEND* (Page 32)
- ½ cup (125ml / 4 oz) white wine
- Salt & pepper to taste

EASY COUSCOUS

INGREDIENTS
MAKES 4 SERVINGS

- 1 cup couscous
- 1 ½ cups *VEGETABLE STOCK* (*BROTH*; Page 27)
- Olive oil
- Lemon juice
- Salt & pepper

I discovered couscous when I lived in the South of France in my early twenties. Yes! I've been around a bit, haven't I? I had troubles with French at University and my mother got me a private tutor. We became really good friends. She was very generous, inviting me to go with her and live with her family until my French was fluent. It was the first time I crossed the border. We took the trip by train. I had such a lovely time! We had dinner with some friends and a couscous salad was served. I asked what it was and I got the explanation that it was an influence from the Maghribian immigrants in France. Interestingly enough, I learned to make couscous in Australia. My sister-in-law, Suzzana, taught me how to make it. It feels like I have created this recipe travelling around the world!

1. Pour vegetable stock (broth) in a cooking pot
2. Place the pot over high heat and bring the liquid to a boil
3. Take the pot off the heat
4. Add couscous, 1 Tablespoon of olive oil, and a squeeze of fresh lemon juice
5. Stir, cover with a lid, and let set for 10 minutes
6. Uncover and separate couscous with a fork
7. Check for seasoning and serve

Use couscous to make *Tabouleh* or any other Middle Eastern inspired salad. I like serving it with stews and as a side dish with meat and fish.

Fish & Meat

"For dinner parties, I love making an easy cioppino using shrimp, mussels, clams, and a hearty fish that won't fall apart easily."

MEGHAN MARKLE

CLAMS WITH GARLIC & SAFFRON IN WHITE WINE SAUCE

INGREDIENTS
MAKES 4 SERVINGS

- 1 kg (2.2 lb) clams
- 1 Tablespoon *GARLIC & PARSLEY BLEND* (Page 32)
- 1 garlic clove
- 1 pinch saffron threads
- ½ cup white wine
- 1 Tablespoon olive oil
- 1 handful fresh parsley
- Salt & pepper to taste

I love clams. I have been eating them since I was a young girl. We used to catch them from the beach and cook them fresh and it was then that I learned how important it was to clean them well. Trust me, you don't want to find sand in your clams; it will destroy the meal. I am fortunate that both my husband and my daughter really enjoy them. Our dear friend Raj loves them too, I always make an effort to cook them when he is around. I learned from an early age not to serve this dish until seated at the table, otherwise clams would be gone before you sit down. My sister Rosa and my daughter are experts at eating clams. I remember the first time my daughter ate this meal, there was barely a tapa left for me when I got to the table. My first reaction was to be upset but then it made me happy to see how much she liked them, and it reminded me of my sister as children, competing who could eat the most clams the fastest.

1. Place clams in a bowl and cover with water. Add 2 Tablespoons of vinegar and 1 Tablespoon of salt (this will help to get rid of the sand). Remove using tongs and rinse them thoroughly under cold running water. Repeat this process one more time to be sure all the sand is gone
2. Heat a medium to large saucepan (one that has a lid) over medium heat
3. Add 1 Tablespoon of olive oil
4. Cook the *GARLIC & PARSLEY BLEND* together with the garlic and saffron until fragrant, for about 1 minute
5. Add clean, rinsed clams to the pan and pour the wine
6. Season with salt and pepper and add fresh parsley
7. Increase heat to medium-high
8. Cover the saucepan with a lid and cook for 5 minutes or until all clams are open
9. Discard any unopened clams; they won't be good to eat. But wait a few more minutes before you do this. Sometimes it takes longer for them to open. You don't want to waste any; they're delicious!

CLAMS WITH GARLIC & SAFFRON IN WHITE WINE SAUCE (continued)

10. Serve the clams with their sauce and juices in a semi-shallow bowl or platter and place in the middle of the table for everybody to enjoy them
11. Make sure to have plenty of bread to dip the sauce; it's so delicious you won't want to be wasted!

This dish makes a perfect pasta sauce. Keep ½ cup of the water from boiling the pasta and add to the clams before mixing with the cooked pasta. Garnish with extra fresh parsley and drizzle with good quality olive oil. You will have a very nice 'pasta vongole' with a Spanish touch.

— *Fish & Meat* —

ASIAN STYLE BAKED SALMON IN A PARCEL

B aking '*en papillote*' is one of the easiest and most rewarding ways to cook fish. My family love eating salmon. When we lived in Melbourne, Australia we used to have Tuesday Salmon. Every week I bought sustainably farmed Tasmanian salmon while my daughter was in swimming lessons. Ever since we moved to California, we try to eat Sockeye or Coho North Pacific salmon, not particularly on Tuesdays, mainly when any of them are on special. This recipe is one of our favourites and my first Asian influenced recipe. The salmon infuses with the saltiness of the Tamari sauce and the light heat from the ginger and scallions (green / spring onions). We really enjoy pouring the juices over PERFECT WHITE RICE (Page 138).

ASIAN STYLE BAKED SALMON IN A PARCEL (continued)

1. Prepare a piece of aluminium foil 3 times the size of the salmon in length
2. Place a piece of baking (parchment) paper big enough to fit the salmon fillet, so it doesn't touch the foil
3. With the salmon fillet on the paper, fold the foil in the corners as if you were making a parcel
4. Thinly slice each scallion (green / spring onions)
5. Pour 1 Tablespoon of Tamari sauce over the salmon
6. Add the sliced scallion (green / spring onions) and ginger
7. Season with freshly ground pepper
8. Close the foil tightly, making sure there are no open-air pockets
9. Repeat for every salmon fillet
10. Preheat the oven to 200C (400F)
11. Bake the salmon for 10 to 15 minutes, depending on the type of salmon or whether you like it a bit rare. Check my note below (*)
12. Take out of the oven and let the salmon rest for 2 to 5 minutes before serving

To serve, open each parcel, place salmon over a bed of white rice and pour the juices over the fish. Sauté a few Asian greens with garlic and ginger and you will have a perfect and balanced meal.

(*) This recipe is based on Atlantic salmon, which is thicker and has more fat than the Sockeye or Coho. If you are using. Sockeye, bake for 8 to 10 minutes only and rest it for 2 minutes maximum. For Coho, bake it for 10 to 12 minutes, depending on how rare you like your salmon.

INGREDIENTS
MAKES 4 SERVINGS

- 4 x 250gr (0.55 lb) fresh salmon fillets
- 4 Tablespoons Tamari sauce (or Soy)
- 4 scallions (green / spring onions) (one for each fillet) including green part
- 4 teaspoons fresh grated ginger or paste
- Freshly ground black pepper to taste
- Aluminium foil
- Baking (parchment) paper

Fish & Meat

EMPANADA GALLEGA (GALICIAN TUNA PIE)

INGREDIENTS

MAKES 4 TO 6 SERVINGS

FOR THE DOUGH

- 500gr (3 ⅓ cups / 1.1 lbs) plain (all-purpose) flour
- ½ cup (125ml / 4 oz) water
- 2 Tablespoons white wine
- 1 cup olive oil (250ml / 8 oz)
- 1 teaspoon salt
- 1 egg

I started making this pie after I heard my friend Salvador speaking about how his mother used to cook it for him in Argentina. I found a suitable recipe and started playing with it until I made it my own. When Salvador's birthday was coming up, I started thinking about what we could give him as a present. Then I remembered! I made him an *empanada gallega* trying to match the one he described from his mum. I placed it in a gift box and gave it to him to open at home. His lovely wife Carla (*CUCUMBER & FRESH MINT SALAD*, Page 95), my dear friend, told me that I had truly surprised him. I couldn't be happier. This is a clear example of the power of food.

TO MAKE THE DOUGH:

1. Place flour and salt in a food processor and pulse a couple of times; or mix by hand in a bowl
2. Add egg, oil, water, wine and pulse until dough is formed; or mix by hand
3. Place the dough on a floured surface and knead until soft and homogeneous (You can also use a stand mixer to make the dough)
4. Divide the dough into 2 balls, wrap with a tea towel, and let it rest until the filling is ready

TO MAKE THE FILLING:

1. Boil the eggs and reserve
2. Finely chop the onion, green capsicum (bell pepper), and garlic
3. Heat 1 Tablespoon of the oil kept from draining the tuna, or olive oil, in a casserole over medium heat
4. Poach the onion for about 2 to 3 minutes
5. Add the capsicum (bell pepper), *GARLIC & PARSLEY BLEND*, and garlic and cook for 5 minutes, or until they are soft
6. Add the tomato, season with salt and pepper, stir in the paprika and cook for 15 minutes, until all liquid is reduced
7. Remove from the heat, leave the sauce to cool, and reserve

EMPANADA GALLEGA (GALICIAN TUNA PIE)
(continued)

INGREDIENTS

FOR THE FILLING

- 480gr (1 lb / 16 oz) canned tuna or canned bonito, well-drained (keep oil for frying, if any)
- 1 onion
- ½ green capsicum (bell pepper)
- 1 Tablespoon *GARLIC & PARSLEY BLEND* (Page 32)
- 1 garlic clove
- 1 x 400gr (11 oz) tin (can) chopped tomatoes
- 12 red pepper stuffed green olives, cut in half
- 4 small fire-roasted red peppers from a jar, roughly broken into thin strips
- 2 hard-boiled eggs
- Salt & pepper to taste
- 1 teaspoon Spanish smoked paprika

8. Chop the boiled eggs
9. Crumble the tuna

TO ASSEMBLE THE PIE:

1. Preheat the oven to 200C (400F)
2. Roll the dough into 2 disks, making sure they overlay the pie pan so that you can seal the pie
3. Place 1 disk on the pie pan and prick using a fork
4. Fill the pie in layers in this order: tomato sauce, crumbled tuna, red peppers in thin strips, olives, and chopped eggs
5. Cover with the second dough disk, folding the edges carefully to close the pastry
6. Paint the top of the pastry with an egg wash
7. Bake pie for approximately 45 minutes or until golden
8. Take out of the oven and serve hot or cold

Serve cut in wedges with a *GREEN SALAD* (Page 94) or *ROASTED ASPARAGUS* (Page 105), when these are in season.

Although this is a traditional fish pie, substitute the crumbled tuna for thinly sliced jarred artichokes hearts for a *VEGETARIAN* version. You will love the combination of flavours.

This pie is traditionally shaped like a big empanada.

Fish & Meat

MUSSELS IN SPICY TOMATO SAUCE

My only problem with cooking mussels is cleaning them. I admit this is the reason I don't cook them often enough. Let me tell you a story about cleaning mussels: on my first camping trip in Australia to Wilsons Promontory National Park (one of the most beautiful places on earth!), my friend Rinaldo, a camping expert, went fishing for local mussels. He brought a bucket full of them. These mussels were smaller than your usual and being fresh from the rocks, very dirty. I lost count of how many mussels I cleaned that day! We all did and kept going with the promise that our dinner was going to be epic… and it was! Rinaldo cooked his dad's signature mussel's pasta sauce. I remember eating around the fire in the open air. All you could hear was the night animals, the sea, and all of us (Cristian, Raj, Daria, Bryan) making sounds of pleasure as we ate. My humble recipe is a simpler and less elaborate dish, but surely full of flavour and very fresh. I hope you agree with me.

1. Scrub the mussels, remove their beards, and rinse thoroughly
2. Place a heavy bottom pot over medium heat and add the olive oil
3. Chop chilli (if using fresh)
4. Cook *PARSLEY & GARLIC BLEND*, chilli, and saffron for 2 minutes
5. Add mussels, tomatoes, and wine (in this order)
6. Season with salt and pepper
7. Shake the pot and cover with a lid
8. Increase heat to medium-high and cook mussels for 10 to 12 minutes, or until most of them are opened
9. Serve mussels with the sauce on a serving bowl or deep platter
10. Discard any unopened mussels
11. Check for seasoning
12. Enjoy!

I like serving this dish over a bed of *PERFECT WHITE RICE* (Page 138) to soak up all the beautiful juices from the sauce. Make sure you have plenty of bread to dip the sauce and a *GREEN SALAD* (Page 94) for colour contrast and crunchiness.

INGREDIENTS
MAKES 4 SERVINGS

- 1kg (2.2 lb / 35.2 oz) fresh mussels
- 2 Tablespoons *GARLIC & PARSLEY BLEND* (Page 32)
- 1 small chilli (or ¼ teaspoon chilli flakes / crushed chilli peppers)
- 1 Tablespoon extra virgin olive oil
- 1 pinch saffron threads
- ½ cup white wine
- 1 tin (can) crushed tomatoes (400gr / 14.5 oz)
- Salt & pepper to taste

BAKED TROUT WITH SERRANO HAM

INGREDIENTS

MAKES 4 SERVINGS

- 4 small to medium fully cleaned trouts
- 8 thin slices of Serrano Ham (or Prosciutto)
- 2 lemons
- Salt & pepper to taste

This is one of my mum's favourite recipes and the only one I'm including in this book from her. In fact, I never considered my mother to be a great cook, but she surely put lots of effort and always bought the best ingredients. Now you know where I get it from, right? She always mentioned how the fat from the Serrano Ham infuses the inside of the trout, making it juicier and saltier. It's true, the flavours combine perfectly. Trouts are now widely available and reasonably priced. You can even catch them yourself. My family once caught our own trouts, although I must admit I prefer to get them from my fishmonger. Not only do I have a nice chat with them, but they also do a better job at cleaning and scaling the fish. Trouts can be quite slippery; I recommend that you use kitchen paper or a tea towel to handle them.

1. Wash the trouts thoroughly and dry with kitchen paper or a tea towel
2. Lay 2 slices of Serrano Ham into each trout, covering the whole belly cavity
3. Freely season the fish with salt and freshly ground pepper (trout skin is quite thick, don't be scared of over-salting it)
4. Cut lemons in half
5. Preheat the oven to 200C (400F)
6. Place trouts on a baking tray (sheet pan) lined with baking (parchment) paper
7. Place lemons with flesh side down
8. Bake trouts and lemons for 10 minutes
9. When the eyes of the fish are opaque white, the fish is cooked (this goes for any type of fish). You can also double check by pulling the meat from the thickest part away from the bone
10. If the trouts are not fully cooked, bake for 2 extra minutes. Fish needs to be nice and moist. Remember it will keep cooking with its internal heat
11. To serve, remove the Serrano ham from the inside of the trouts and place on each dinner plate

BAKED TROUT WITH SERRANO HAM (continued)

12. Prepare the trouts by removing the skin. Fillet the trout carefully, making sure you take off all the bones (as many as you can). Now pull the whole bone structure and clean the rest of the flesh. This bottom part will be easier to prepare
13. Place trout meat on each serving plate, next to the Serrano ham, with a piece of the baked lemon
14. To eat, squeeze the lemon over the fish meat and take a piece of trout and a piece of Serrano ham. Delicious!

You can serve this simple fish with any of the salads and/or side dishes in this book.

Fish & Meat

SUNG CHOI BAO

Also known as *'lettuce wraps'*, this Chinese dish is a regular at my organic kitchen. Living in Australia has opened my culinary horizons, and Chinese cuisine has become one of my favourites. I find this dish easy and quick to prepare and it is full of flavour and lots of fun to eat. My daughter loves eating it with *PERFECT WHITE RICE* (Page 138). It is one of her preferred meals to take for school lunch. Traditionally served with iceberg lettuce, I like to serve it with butter lettuce. I find that its texture and flavour complement the meat mixture very well, making it very tasty and easier to eat. Let's face it: this is a messy meal to eat, but that's what makes it so fun. The combination of beef and turkey creates a softer and juicier wrap.

1. Cut the core of the lettuce and soak the leaves in cold water until ready to serve
2. Finely chop garlic, ginger, and carrot in a food processor
3. Mix Oyster and Tamari sauces and Sesame oil with the stock (broth)
4. Preheat a wok or deep saucepan with 1 Tablespoon of oil over medium-high heat
5. Crumble half of the mince into the wok or saucepan and cook until all liquid has evaporated and is well browned
6. Remove the first batch and reheat the wok
7. Cook the remaining meat, remove and reserve
8. Reheat the wok or saucepan on medium heat and add 1 Tablespoon of oil
9. Stir fry garlic, ginger, and carrots for 1 minute
10. Return mince to the wok or saucepan and mix for another minute
11. Make a well in the centre, pour the sauces and broth (stock) mix and stir to blend
12. Add bean sprouts, spring / green onions (scallions), coriander (cilantro) and toss to combine
13. Sprinkle with sesame seeds
14. Dry lettuce leaves
15. Spoon mince mixture into each leaf and roll up to make a little parcel
16. Eat with your hands and enjoy!

Create your own *PLANT-BASED* version by stir-frying colourful vegetables cut into strips.

INGREDIENTS
MAKES 4 TO 6 SERVINGS

- ½ kg (1.1 lb) minced (ground) beef
- ½ kg (1.1 lb) minced (ground) turkey thigh (or chicken)
- 2 Tablespoons olive oil
- 4 garlic cloves, smashed and peeled
- 8cm (3") piece fresh ginger (or 1 Tablespoon ginger paste)
- 1 large carrot
- ½ bunch scallions (spring / green onions), slice diagonally, including green part
- 2 Tablespoons each **Oyster** and **Tamari** **sauce** (or Soy)
- 1 teaspoon Sesame Oil
- 1 cup (250ml / 8 oz) chicken or vegetable stock (broth)
- 2 handfuls bean sprouts
- 1 handful fresh coriander (cilantro), roughly chopped
- 1 butter lettuce
- 1 Tablespoon sesame seeds
- Salt & pepper to taste

Fish & Meat

BUTTER CHICKEN

Butter chicken came into my organic kitchen after we moved to Northern California. I had time to explore and develop new recipes, plus I LOVED COOKING in the wonderful kitchen at our first accommodation! After a few times, I feel I have created a nice recipe, with quite an authentic Indian Balti flavour. It was my daughter's friend, Lila's, preferred dish when she first came over. Lila was my daughter's first friend in California, and they are still besties, as I am with her mum, even before we landed in the US. I like calling this dish *Lila's butter chicken*.

1. Make the [marinade](#) by mixing all ingredients until well combined
2. Clean chicken pieces of any fat and place them into a large pot or bowl with a lid
3. Pour marinade over the chicken, cover and place in the fridge overnight, or at least for ½ day
4. Before you start cooking, take the chicken out of the fridge to reach room temperature (about 30 minutes to 1 hour ahead)

TO MAKE THE SAUCE & FINAL RECIPE:

1. Lightly toast coriander and fennel seeds in a pan over a gentle heat until fragrant
2. Place toasted seeds, garlic cloves, fresh ginger, almonds, tomatoes, salt, and peppercorns in a food processor and blend to a smooth consistency
3. Put your favourite cooking pot or wok over medium heat, add 1 Tablespoon of oil and cook chicken thigh fillets, 2 minutes each side, until brown. Do this in batches and keep them warm
4. Cut the onions in quarters and then slice thinly
5. Add 1 more Tablespoon of oil to the cooking pot or wok and fry onions for about 3 minutes on medium heat
6. Cut chicken fillets into bite sizes, add to the pot, and stir with the onion
7. Pour the sauce over the chicken and mix well
8. Cover the pot and cook over medium heat for about 10 minutes

INGREDIENTS
MAKES 4 TO 6 SERVINGS

- 1kg (2.2 lb) chicken thigh fillets

MARINADE

- ⅔ cup (160ml / 5 oz) natural (plain) yogurt
- Juice of 1 lemon
- ½ teaspoon cayenne pepper or chilli powder
- 1 teaspoon ground cumin
- 1 teaspoon ground coriander
- 1 teaspoon garam masala
- 1 teaspoon turmeric
- 1 teaspoon salt
- Black pepper

Fish & Meat

BUTTER CHICKEN (continued)

INGREDIENTS

SAUCE AND FINAL RECIPE

- 2 Tablespoons extra virgin olive oil (you can also use butter or ghee; or a combination)
- 2 medium brown onions
- 1 Tablespoon coriander seeds
- 1 Tablespoon fennel seeds
- 2 garlic cloves
- 2cm (0.75") piece fresh ginger
- 50gr (1.75 oz / ¼ cup) almonds (any almond that you have in your pantry)
- 1 tin (can) tomato puree (400gr / 14.5 oz)
- 1 teaspoon salt
- ¼ teaspoon black peppercorns
- 4 Tablespoons butter
- Fresh cilantro (coriander) to garnish

9. To finish the dish, add 4 Tablespoons of butter, let them melt and stir until well combined
10. Garnish with fresh roughly chopped coriander (cilantro) and check for seasoning before serving

It may seem complicated, but trust me, it is easier than it sounds, and it tastes wonderful!

Serve it with *PERFECT WHITE RICE* (Page 138), *PARATHA* (Page 194), and *CUCUMBER & MINT SALAD* (Page 95).

For an Indian-style banquet add *DHAL* (Page 125) to the menu. Your loved ones will be transported to the streets of Delhi. You will also cater for any *VEGETARIAN*.

To make it *DAIRY-FREE* substitute the yogurt for coconut cream and butter for coconut oil. The coconut flavour really compliments this dish.

OSSOBUCO STEW WITH ZUCCHINI & PUMPKIN

Ossobuco or *osso buco* is Italian for 'bone with a hole' (*osso* 'bone', *buco* 'hole'), a reference to the bone marrow in this cut of meat. Usually a cheap cut, I was very surprised at its high price when I bought it for the first time in Northern California. Introduced to me as a hearty soup, I have developed this recipe into a stew. Who doesn't love a warm stew on a cold day? This dish is full of flavour. I love the sauce that forms from the pumpkin and bone marrow. I remember one cold Monday night after my husband played guitar with his friends and they came home to this wonderful stew. It warmed their souls after walking in Melbourne winter weather; the cold goes through your bones!

1. Trim the meat from the bones and cut into bite-size pieces
2. Place a heavy bottom pot over medium-high heat
3. Add 1 Tablespoon of olive oil
4. Brown *ossobuco* and its bones and reserve; do this in batches. Add a little extra oil if needed
5. Wash carrots and celery
6. Peel and chop onion and carrots
7. Thinly slice celery
8. Heat another Tablespoon of olive oil
9. Add onion, carrots, and celery and toss through for 3 minutes
10. Reduce heat to medium
11. Crush, peel and chop garlic and sauté with vegetables for 1 minute
12. Add dry oregano, stir and fry for 1 more minute
13. Return meat to the pot
14. Peel and cut the pumpkin into cubes
15. Add pumpkin to the pot and mix well
16. Wash and cut zucchini in 4 long strips and slice
17. Add zucchini and tomatoes to the pot
18. Season with salt and pepper
19. Pour stock (broth) and shake the pot

INGREDIENTS
MAKES 6 SERVINGS

- 1kg (2.2 lb) ossobuco (beef shin)
- 1 medium to large red onion
- 2 garlic cloves
- 2 medium carrots
- 2 celery sticks
- 340gr (0.75 lb / 12 oz) butternut pumpkin
- 2 medium zucchinis (courgettes)
- 1 tin (can) crushed or chopped tomatoes (400gr / 14.5 oz)
- 1 cup CHICKEN STOCK (BROTH; Page 28)
- 2 teaspoons dry oregano
- Olive oil
- Salt & pepper to taste

OSSOBUCO STEW WITH ZUCCHINI & PUMPKIN
(continued)

20. Bring stew to the boil, reduce heat to low, cover and simmer for 30 minutes
21. Check seasoning and dryness. Add ¼ to ½ cup of stock (broth or water) if the stew looks dry
22. Cook 15 to 30 minutes extra, depending on how tender you prefer the meat (the longer you cook it the more flavour will have)
23. Let rest for 10 minutes off the heat
24. Scoop out bone marrow from bones and mix through the stew. This will help break the pumpkin and create a creamier dish (Yum!)
25. You can discard the bones now

Serve over *PERFECT WHITE RICE* (Page 138), *EASY COUSCOUS* (page 150), or *BASIC QUINOA* (Page 36) and a *CUCUMBER & FRESH MINT SALAD* (PAGE 95).

Your loved ones are going to ask you to cook this stew all the time!

This is a perfect dish to cook in a *PRESSURE COOKER* or *INSTANT POT*. Once you bring the stew to the boil, cover and cook on high for 30 minutes, with a quick steam release. Let rest for 15 minutes before serving. Follow your *INSTANT POT* instructions for cooking stews.

Fish & Meat

BUTTERFLY ROASTED CHICKEN WITH LEMON, GARLIC & ROSEMARY

As Julia Child said: "*Roast chicken has always been one of life's great pleasures.*" I find that lemon goes really well with chicken and the addition of garlic and rosemary is a match made in heaven. This recipe is my interpretation of Salvador's grilled butterfly chicken. My lovely father-in-law is one of the best *asadores* I know. He takes pride in his Argentinean heritage and he's the king of the BBQ wherever he goes. I have watched him countless times making this chicken and I'm grateful to have made it my own. Well, I must admit, my husband started cooking it at home first, although he cooks it under the oven grill (broiler). I prefer to roast this butterfly chicken. I find it cooks more evenly than a whole chicken. Although I use mainly dry herbs in most recipes in this book, I encourage you to use fresh Rosemary in this recipe. The difference in flavour is worth to have a plant or ask your neighbour for a strand.

BUTTERFLY ROASTED CHICKEN WITH LEMON, GARLIC & ROSEMARY (continued)

1. Melt the butter on low heat
2. Crush, peel and thinly chop the garlic
3. Chop the rosemary
4. Juice the whole lemon
5. Make the marinade by mixing the melted butter, garlic, lemon, and rosemary
6. Clean the chicken thoroughly, mainly the inside cavity, and pat dry
7. Place chicken on a chopping board with the breast side down
8. Using kitchen scissors or chicken shears, cut along the backbone
9. Pat dry the inside of the chicken and brush a bit of the marinade; season with salt and pepper
10. Lay a roasting pan (baking sheet) with baking (parchment) paper
11. Place the chicken with the breast side up on the tray and press down firmly on the breast bone to flatten the chicken
12. Brush the whole chicken with the marinade, add salt and pepper
13. Preheat the oven to 200C (400F)
14. When the oven is ready, bake the chicken for 45 minutes to 1 hour (this will depend on the size of the chicken)
15. Check after 45 minutes by inserting a sharp knife between the leg and the breast. If the liquid runs clear, the chicken is cooked.
16. Bigger chickens will take longer to bake
17. Once baked, take the chicken out of the oven and let rest for 15 minutes before carving and serving

This is a very comforting meal. Serve with any salad or side dish from this book.

I like making this chicken as one sheet pan dinner by putting root vegetables around the bird (carrots, parsnips, fennel, golden beets). The juices of the chicken and the marinade make the vegetables a delicacy to eat. I prepare this dinner whenever I'm coming home late and want to have a cooked meal. I program the oven, so that the chicken is ready when I walk through the door. You will love the smell!

INGREDIENTS

MAKES 4 TO 6 SERVINGS

- 1 whole chicken (1.5kg – 2kg / 3.3 – 4.4 lbs) preferably organic free-range
- 1 lemon
- 4 cloves garlic
- 4 Tablespoons salted butter (50gr approximately)
- 1 Tablespoon fresh rosemary (or 1 teaspoon dry)
- 1 teaspoon salt (or to taste)
- Freshly ground black pepper

Fish & Meat

CHILI CON 'CARMEN'

INGREDIENTS

MAKES 4 TO 6 SERVINGS

- 1kg (2.2 lb) minced (ground) beef
- 1 medium red onion, finely chopped
- 1 poblano pepper or green capsicum, chopped
- 1 jalapeño pepper or fresh chilli, finely chopped
- 2 garlic cloves, finely chopped
- 1 x 400gr (11 oz) tin (can) chopped tomatoes
- 1 x 400gr (11 oz) tin (can) pinto (or black) beans
- 2 cups (500ml / 16 oz) chicken or vegetable stock (broth)
- 1 teaspoon chilli powder or ½ teaspoon cayenne pepper
- 1 teaspoon each ground **cumin**, **paprika** and dry **oregano**
- 1 bay leaf
- 2 Tablespoons cornmeal (or polenta)
- 1 to 2 Tablespoons olive oil
- Salt & pepper to taste

My friend Remko loves Mexican food. It seemed that whenever he came to visit, I always cooked chili con carne. That's why he named this recipe "*chili con Carmen*", to make a point about me always cooking the same meal for him! Although embarrassed at first, I saw the humour in the situation and today I'm grateful for calling my famous Mexican meal with my first name. I met Remko through my dear friend Nikkie. They are a lovely couple with a great sense of humour and they are fantastic musicians.

1. Heat 1 Tablespoon of oil in a large heavy-based pot or saucepan
2. Cook meat until browned and reserve; you can do this in batches
3. Add more oil, if needed, and sauté onion and pepper (capsicum) until soft, for about 3 minutes
4. Add garlic and jalapeño, or chilli, and fry for 2 more minutes
5. Pour tomatoes and stir until well combined
6. Add spices, one at a time, mixing constantly to evenly distribute the flavours
7. Return meat to the pot and mix in the cornmeal (or polenta)
8. Add beans, broth (stock), and bay leaf
9. Check for seasoning and bring to the boil
10. Reduce heat and simmer for 1 hour
11. Before serving, remove bay leaf and check for seasoning again

Serve with PERFECT WHITE RICE (Page 138), SIMPLE GUACAMOLE (Page 72), and Mexican tortilla chips (*totopos*).

This recipe is perfect for PRESSURE COOKING and INSTANT POT. Add only ½ **CUP** of broth (stock) and cook on high setting for 15 minutes. For better results, use slow steam release and allow resting for 15 minutes before serving.

PUMPKIN CHILLI is a delicious PLANT-BASED dish. Substitute the meat for pumpkin cut into dice bite-size pieces, add it to the pot with the beans and 1 **CUP** vegetable stock (broth), and reduce cooking time to ½ hour. (Check the recipe on my blog. Use the QR code at the end of this book).

ROAST ARGENTINIAN ASADO WITH CHIMICHURRI

Married to an Argentinean, I have eaten plenty of asados. Making asado is an art. Asado is traditionally cooked over charcoal. My father-in-law and my husband are great 'asadores'. This recipe came to me when I celebrated my first Christmas Eve in California. We invited our new Danish friends. We met Ole, Carina and their beautiful children at our first Thanksgiving Dinner in the USA at my long time and dearest friend Daria's. I wanted to showcase our family heritage through food. Thus, I made tapas as starters, asado with *chimichurri* as the main meal and *PAVLOVA* (Page 219) as dessert. My husband wasn't happy with my first attempt at roasting asado! He has been fully involved in developing this recipe. You can be sure it is as close as it can get to the real thing.

INGREDIENTS
MAKES 4 SERVINGS

- 1 Kg (2.2 lb) beef short ribs
- 2 Tablespoons olive oil
- Salt
- Freshly ground black pepper to taste

1. Brush all ribs with olive oil
2. Add plenty of salt and pepper on all the sides
3. Place ribs on the bone side on an oven-safe tray or shallow pot and seal on medium-high heat for 5 minutes (the bone marrow should get black, to make sure the bone is cooked through)
4. Preheat the oven to 180C (350F)
5. Bake short ribs for 45 minutes
6. Increase oven temperature to 200C (400F) and bake for 15 extra minutes
7. Transfer the meat onto a clean tray and out of the oven and let it rest for 10 to 15 minutes before serving
8. Serve a piece of short rib per guest with 1 Tablespoon of *chimichurri* (Page 178) over the meat and be ready for the silence

ROAST ARGENTINIAN ASADO WITH CHIMICHURRI
(continued)

INGREDIENTS
CONTINUED

CHIMICHURRI

MAKES 1 ¼ CUP

- 1 medium red capsicum (bell pepper)
- 2 garlic cloves
- ½ teaspoon salt
- 6 whole peppercorns
- ½ bunch fresh parsley
- 2 teaspoons apple cider vinegar
- ⅔ cup (160ml / 5 oz) extra virgin olive oil
- ½ teaspoon ground cumin
- ½ teaspoon smoked Spanish paprika
- ¼ teaspoon cayenne pepper
- 2 teaspoons dry oregano

TO MAKE THE CHIMICHURRI:

1. Mash garlic over salt and peppercorns in a mortar and pestle until it forms a paste
2. Cut the capsicum (bell pepper) into thin strips and then chop into small cubes
3. Finely chop the parsley, including the stems; you can do this using a food processor
4. In a bowl, add all dry ingredients (cumin, paprika, cayenne pepper, and oregano) and mix well
5. Add parsley, bell pepper (capsicum), and garlic paste and blend through
6. Pour in olive oil and vinegar and stir until all ingredients are well combined
7. Taste with a piece of bread (this is the preferred way) and fix seasoning to your liking
8. *Chimichurri* gets better with time. Keep it in the fridge in an airtight container or glass (mason) jar

Chimichurri is a great fresh sauce to add to any meat. It is great with hot dogs and sausages. Across Argentina, you can find different ways to make it. This recipe is my favourite. I love the freshness of the red capsicum (bell pepper).

To make PLANT-BASED ASADO, marinate firm tofu with *chimichurri* and keep in the fridge for a few hours. Grill the tofu over medium heat on both sides. I assure you that you have a winning dish. I made it once for my friend Lesley at one asado and she said it was the tastiest tofu she had ever eaten!

Whenever you eat red meat, make sure to have plenty of greens as side dishes. Argentinians eat asado with fries, potatoes and carrot salad with mayonnaise, and a plain green salad.

Bread & Pizza

"No matter what the recipe, any baker can do wonders in the kitchen with some good ingredients and an upbeat attitude!"

BUDDY VALASTRO

EASY FLATBREAD

I learned to make bread at the *Convent Bakery* in Melbourne, Australia. My husband and my daughter gave me the course as a Mother's Day present. I loved the experience; even though I had to get up very early one Sunday morning. But I got to see hot air balloons in the air! I had made bread before, but I wanted to learn from the experts how to make it better. Ever since, I have tested making different types of bread and using different types of flour. This flatbread is my go-to recipe when I want to have warm bread out of the oven to serve with soups or when friends come over. It is very quick to put together and it bakes while you're setting up the table. It is a crowd-pleaser and one that I am asked to make all the time.

1. Place milk, water, and yeast in a small saucepan over low heat and stir until lukewarm; set aside
2. Mix flours and salt in a large bowl and make a well
3. Pour yeast mixture and olive oil, and mix until a smooth dough forms
4. Knead on a lightly floured surface for 5 minutes
5. Add a little extra flour if the dough is too sticky
6. You can do this using a stand or hand mixer fitted with the hook attachment (this is how I do it)
7. Oil a bowl, sprinkle semolina, and place the dough
8. Cover with a tea towel and let your dough rise for 30 minutes, until it has doubled in size
9. Preheat the oven to 200C (400F)
10. Brush the baking tray with oil and sprinkle semolina
11. Drop bread dough into the prepared baking tray
12. Oil your hands and gently flatten the dough using the palms of your hands until it reaches the edges of the tray and it has the same thickness all over
13. Brush dough with extra olive oil and sprinkle rosemary or thyme and plenty of salt
14. Bake for 20 minutes
15. Let stand in the tray for 5 minutes
16. Cut into pieces and serve on a wooden board

Experiment with different flours and toppings but remember this is not *focaccia*. This dough works really well as individual small dinner rolls. They are delicious served warm out of the oven. Yum!

INGREDIENTS
FOR A 32 X 22cm (13" X 9") BAKING TRAY

- 1 ⅓ cup spelt flour (200gr / 0.44 lb / 7 oz)
- 1 cup semolina flour (150gr / 0.33 lb / 5.3oz)
- ⅓ cup plain (all-purpose or bread) flour (50gr / 0.11 lb / 1.7 oz)
- 2 teaspoons dry yeast (or a sachet 7gr / ¼ oz)
- ¾ cup milk (180ml / 6 oz)
- ½ cup water (125ml / 4 oz)
- 1 Tablespoon olive oil
- 1 teaspoon salt

BASIC WHOLEMEAL BREAD

INGREDIENTS

MAKES 1 LOAF

- 1 cup (250ml / 8 oz) homemade buttermilk at room temperature (*TIPS & TRICKS*; Page 19)
- ⅔ cup (160ml / 5 oz) lukewarm water
- 2 teaspoons dry yeast or 1 packet (7gr / ¼ oz)
- 1 ½ cups (225gr / 0.5 lb) wholemeal (whole-wheat) flour
- 2/3 cup (100gr / 0.22 lb) plain (all-purpose or bread) flour
- 1 cup (150gr / 0.33 lb) semolina flour
- 1 Tablespoon olive oil
- 1 teaspoon salt

This bread is perfect for sandwiches and toasts. You can use any flour (except *gluten-free*) and even add seeds, olives or dried fruit. I like the texture and flavour of wholemeal (whole-wheat) flour. I always have a loaf of this bread at home. Sometimes I make double and keep one in the freezer. I use my stand mixer to make bread, which is easier for my hands, cleaner and quicker. However, I always do a final kneading by hand; I find it very therapeutic, plus it adds elasticity to the bread. The instructions below are for the full hands-on bread making experience, which I advise you try at least once. Children love manipulating dough; they will enjoy the experience and help you when the gluten starts to activate and the dough gets harder. Make sure they do not overwork the dough, or you will end up with very tough bread. I'm sure you will be making bread more often than you ever thought you would.

1. Mix buttermilk and water in a bowl; add the yeast and stir until well dissolved
2. Mix flours with salt in another bowl, make a well in the centre and pour in the butter milk, water and yeast mixture
3. Slowly add olive oil and mix until a soft and sticky dough is formed
4. Oil your hands and turn the dough onto a lightly oiled surface. Knead for 5 minutes
5. Let the dough rest for 5 minutes (this is a very important step; it allows the dough to relax). Knead again for 5 more minutes
6. Lightly oil a large bowl and sprinkle semolina. Place dough in the bowl, cover with a tea towel and leave to rise for 30 minutes to 1 hour, until it doubles in size
7. Grease a loaf (bread) tin with oil and a sprinkle of semolina
8. Oil your hands again, place the dough on a lightly oiled surface and punch down softly into a rectangular shape. Roll up from the short end to create the loaf
9. Place the dough in the tin with the seam side down and tuck the ends underneath

BASIC WHOLEMEAL BREAD (continued)

10. Spray with water and sprinkle some flour for a rustic and bakery look
11. Place in a cold oven and set the temperature to 220C (425F). Bake for 30 minutes (read my note bellow)
12. Reduce temperature to 200C (400F) and bake for 20 to 25 minutes more, until the loaf sounds hollow when removed from the baking tin and tapped on the base
13. Let rest for 5 minutes in the bread tin
14. Place on a wire rack to cool completely

I have shared my tip for saving the second leavening (proofing) of the bread. I like it because it speeds the baking time. However, if you have time and for better results, take the time to rise your bread after you have placed it in the tin loaf for extra 30 minutes to 1 hour, until it has doubled in size. Preheat the oven to 200C (400F) and bake the loaf for 40 to 45 minutes and it sounds hollow when tapped at the bottom.

— Bread & Pizza —

CHALLAH

The word *Challah* is Biblical in origin. This special bread in Jewish cuisine is usually braided and typically eaten on ceremonial occasions. Pronounced Hallah (haa·luh), this bread is great for French toasts, better than brioche in my humble opinion, with no intention to offend anybody. This recipe is the result of me testing a traditional Jewish recipe that was given to me by my friend, Romina. She has attended some of my Spanish-speaking cooking classes. We both share our connection with Argentina and our love for our dear friend Aurora. They're united by soccer, their children and their great attitude towards life.

1. In a large bowl (or the bowl of your stand mixer), dissolve the yeast with warm water and sugar. Let rest for 5 to 10 minutes, until it turns foamy
2. Add 1 cup of flour (150gr) and start mixing
3. Beat the egg with the oil and salt

CHALLAH (continued)

4. Add egg mixture to the bowl and blend
5. Add the remaining flour and mix until you have a smooth dough
6. Turn the dough onto a lightly floured surface and knead for 5 minutes (or use your stand mixer with the hook attachment)
7. Lightly oil a large bowl and sprinkle with semolina
8. Place dough in the bowl, cover tightly with a tea towel, and allow to rise for 1 to 2 hours
9. Preheat the oven to 180C (350F)
10. Gently punch down the risen dough and turn out onto a lightly floured counter
11. Divide the dough into 3 equal parts and roll into logs, about 3.8cm (1.5") thick and 40cm (16") long
12. Pinch the ends of the three logs together firmly and braid from the middle until to complete the loaf
13. Line a baking tray with parchment (baking) paper and a sprinkle of semolina flour
14. Place the shaped *Challah* on the tray and brush with the egg wash
15. Bake for 25 to 30 minutes, until golden brown
16. Let the bread rest for 5 minutes on the baking tray
17. Place on a wire rack to cool completely

For better results, proof the braided *Challah* a second time, until it doubles in size (about 30 minutes to 1 hour) and then bake as indicated above.

Use this *Challah* bread to make FRENCH TOAST (Page 61), as breakfast sweet bread or to share at celebrations. As Marnie Winston-Macauley says: *"Challah stands alone (except for maybe some raisins, and French toast) – and should be dosed straight, with love, and respect."*

INGREDIENTS
MAKES 1 LOAF

- ⅓ + ¼ cup (140ml / 4.7 oz) warm water
- 1.5 teaspoons dry yeast
- ⅓ cup (70gr / 2.5 oz) raw sugar
- 1 egg
- 300gr (2 cups / 0.66 lb / 10.58 oz) plain (all-purpose) flour
- 2 Tablespoons olive oil
- 1 teaspoon salt
- 1 egg yolk mixed with 1 Tablespoon of water for brushing (Use egg white to make STRAWBERRY & BASIL SORBET; Page 216)

PANE DI CASA

INGREDIENTS

MAKES 1 LOAF

- 300ml (1 ¼ cup approximately / 10.15 oz) cold filtered water
- 0.5 teaspoon dry yeast
- 250gr (1 ⅔ cup / 0.55 lb) plain (all-purpose or bread) flour
- 250gr (1 ⅔ cup / 0.55 lb) semolina flour
- 1 Tablespoon olive oil
- 1 teaspoon salt

Pane di casa translates as *homemade bread*. I feel very fortunate to have this recipe. This is the bread that I used to buy at my local bakery in Melbourne, Australia. The baker that ran the bread making course that I attended had been a manager at that bakery and shared this loaf recipe. This bread is very rustic and wholesome. I love the fact that it uses very little yeast. Because it proofs overnight, the flavour intensifies and it's a delicious bread. This is the perfect bread to bake on the weekend. I always had a few loaves of *Spelt Pane di Casa* to sell in my market stalls. They used to sell out very quickly. I remember teaching my dear friend Mariana to make this bread. What an amazing kneader! She doesn't need any machine! Introduced through a friend before we were mums, our daughters brought us together. I treasure her friendship and that of our families.

1. In the afternoon, mix all ingredients until you have a smooth dough (use your stand or hand mixer)
2. Turn the dough onto a lightly floured surface and knead for 10 minutes; mould into a ball (or let your machine do the work for you)
3. Lightly oil a large bowl and sprinkle with semolina
4. Place the dough in the bowl, cover tightly with a tea towel and place in the microwave overnight (this ensures that no air will dry out the dough)
5. In the morning, turn the dough onto a lightly floured surface and knock back gently with the palm of your hands
6. Mould into a rectangle
7. Fold in three from one short edge, as if you were making an envelope
8. Gently roll and stretch the dough until you have a Vienna loaf shape (a large rustic looking baguette)
9. Line a baking tray with parchment (baking) paper and sprinkle with semolina
10. Place the shaped dough with the seam down on the prepared baking tray

PANE DI CASA (continued)

11. Cover with a tea towel and put back in the microwave to proof for another hour
12. Preheat the oven to 220C (425F)
13. Score the bread doing 3 to 4 diagonal cuts with a very sharp knife or bread scorer
14. Spray with water and sprinkle some flour for a rustic and bakery look
15. Bake for 20 minutes
16. Reduce oven temperature to 200C (400F) and bake for an additional 20 to 25 minutes, until the loaf sounds hollow when tapped on the base
17. Let the bread rest for 5 minutes on the baking tray
18. Place on a wire rack to cool completely

You will love the texture and flavour of this bread. I recommend that you experiment with other flours. *Rye Pane di Casa* is very nice too. Don't be afraid of not shaping the loaf perfectly, the more rustic looking, the better it will be. Besides, you will get better at it as you continue making it.

SPELT PIZZA DOUGH

I discovered spelt flour when recovering from a health fright, which lasted two years. My naturopath suggested that I avoid refined flours and fermented foods. My love of food made me research alternative flours, so I could still enjoy eating and making pizza at home. Spelt is an ancient grain. It is an excellent source of protein, fibre, B vitamins and some minerals. Spelt flour works as well as plain (all-purpose) flour in most recipes, being a healthier option. The addition of semolina gives this pizza dough a special and crispy texture.

1. Activate the dry yeast with the warm water by mixing well in a bowl and set aside. Luke warm water should be 37 to 40C (90 to 105F)
2. Using a stand mixer fitted with the dough hook, add flours and salt and mix for a few seconds. You can do this process by hand
3. Add the activated yeast with water, olive oil, and mix at medium speed until a compact dough is form, kneading for 5 minutes
4. Place the dough in an oiled bowl and cover with a clean tea towel and let proof for 30 minutes, or until it doubles in size. The best place to proof your dough is inside your microwave oven
5. Oil your hands and form four equal balls of the dough
6. Cut baking (parchment) paper to the same size as the pizza tray or stone, drizzle with olive oil and sprinkle some semolina
7. Preheat the oven to the highest temperature (250 to 280C / 450 to 500F) and place pizza trays or pizza stones to preheat. This ensures a crispy base
8. Roll each ball with a rolling pin or oiled hands over the prepared paper. Top with your favourite toppings
9. With the help of the paper, carefully place the pizzas over the hot tray or stone and bake for 10 to 15 minutes

My family likes thin crust pizzas, but if you prefer a thicker pizza base, divide this recipe into 3 equal parts.

You will never buy pizza out again!

Buon Appetito!

INGREDIENTS
MAKES 4 MEDIUM PIZZAS

- 2 cups spelt flour (300gr / 0.66 lb / 10.6 oz)
- 1 cup semolina flour (150gr / 0.33 lb / 5.3 oz)
- ⅓ cup (50gr / 0.11 lb / 1.8 oz) plain (all-purpose or bread) flour
- 2 teaspoons dry yeast
- 310ml lukewarm water (1 ¼cup / 10 oz)
- 1 Tablespoon olive oil
- 1 teaspoon salt

ZUCCHINI, SAUSAGE & PROVOLONE WHITE PIZZA

INGREDIENTS
MAKES 1 MEDIUM PIZZA

- ¼ or ⅓ Spelt pizza dough (Page 189)
- 1 small zucchini (courgette)
- 1 small mild Italian sausage (or any other of your liking)
- 125gr (¼ lb approximately) provolone cheese
- ½ teaspoon dry thyme
- Extra virgin olive oil
- Salt & pepper to taste

I really like experimenting with different pizza toppings. I saw this pizza in a gourmet section of a famous department store in Madrid, Spain. My cousin Tere and her lovely husband Pedro took our daughters and me the last Christmas we spent with them. The place had opened recently, and they wanted to show it to me. They know me so well; what a foodie's paradise! When I saw the pizza combination, I told my cousin I was going to make it. And so, as soon as I returned to Australia, I did. Sometimes I use different cheeses if I cannot find provolone, but the combination of flavours is very nice. My cousin is like a younger sibling to me. Our connection since childhood is very strong. Even though I've been living abroad for many years, we've managed to stay very close and pass on our strong bond to our daughters and husbands.

1. Wash, pat dry, and grate zucchini with a medium grater (thicker than for grating cheese)
2. Place the grated zucchini on a colander and sprinkle some salt over it
3. Extend pizza dough as per my recipe and brush with olive oil
4. Remove the meat from the sausage casing, make small uneven balls, and place them over the pizza dough
5. Squeeze zucchini and scatter over the pizza, around the sausage pieces
6. Grate the provolone cheese and distribute over the pizza
7. Sprinkle with thyme
8. Drizzle with olive oil and add salt and pepper
9. Bake for 10 to 15 minutes in a preheated very hot oven (250 to 280C / 450 to 500F)

This is a great pizza to make *VEGETARIAN*, just omit the sausage. You will be surprised how nice it tastes!

MANCHEGO, ROASTED PEPPERS & OLIVES PIZZA

This pizza was created out of luck. We took our friend Kristeena's daughter home while she was working. We invited her to stay for dinner when she came to pick her up. I had already made 3 pizzas and I wanted to create a different one. She suggested looking for what I had in the pantry and fridge and make one up. Originally, we added chorizo, but I found this *VEGETARIAN* version much nicer and lighter. Kristeena has been my husband's official barber. We met her at our first school in California. We're very grateful for her friendship.

1. Extend pizza dough as per my recipe
2. Spread *Passata* over the extended pizza dough
3. Grate Manchego cheese and scatter over the pizza
4. Tear the roasted pepper in thin strips and place them all over the pizza
5. Drop olives around the pizza
6. Drizzle with a bit of olive oil
7. Sprinkle with oregano
8. Add salt and pepper
9. Bake for 10 to 15 minutes in a preheated very hot oven (250C+ / 450-500F)

This is one of my favourite pizzas. The Manchego cheese gives a depth of flavour that goes really well with the roasted pepper and olives.

Take it to another level and add Spanish or Italian anchovies in olive oil straight from a jar once the pizza is out of the oven. You will love it!

INGREDIENTS
MAKES 1 MEDIUM PIZZA

- ¼ or ⅓ Spelt pizza dough (Page 189)
- 1 cup *PASSATA* (tomato sauce; Page 37)
- 1 roasted red pepper
- 125gr (¼ lb approximately) Manchego cheese
- 12 olives
- ½ teaspoon dry oregano
- Extra virgin olive oil
- Salt & pepper to taste

PARATHA

INGREDIENTS

MAKES 4 TO 6 SERVINGS

- 300gr (2 cups / 0.66 lb / 10.5 oz) wholemeal (*atta* or whole-wheat) flour
- 200ml (½ + ⅓ cup / 6.8 oz) cold water
- 1 Tablespoon olive oil, plus extra for rolling and cooking
- 1 teaspoon salt

Paratha is a humble Indian flatbread traditionally made with *ATTA* flour. I have seen my dear friend Rajesh roll *Paratha* made by his mum on many occasions. This recipe is my tribute to him and our many Indian meals cooked by his parents. Raj has been my husband's friend for many years. He has been an important part of our journey as a couple from the beginning. He witnessed my Australian permanent residency, was the best man at our wedding, and has been an uncle to our daughter from birth. To me, he is my brother in Australia. He has done things for me that only a brother would do. He inspired me to take on cooking as my artistic expression and write this book.

1. To make the dough, mix flour and salt in a large bowl
2. Make a well in the centre add water slowly and then the oil
3. Mix all ingredients until a sticky dough starts to form
4. Oil your hands and knead the bread for 5 minutes
5. Cover the bowl with a tea towel and rest the dough for 15 minutes (this is very important, as it makes the dough more elastic and easier to work with)
6. This process can be done with a stand mixer, it's quicker and easier
7. Sprinkle flour over your kitchen bench and place the dough
8. Divide the dough into 12 equal pieces
9. Roll out each piece until thin, brush with some oil and fold in three as if you were folding a letter before putting it in an envelope
10. Fold again in three until you have a small square; we are building the layers
11. Scrunch each piece of dough into a ball; this keeps the oil inside
12. Roll out each ball until you get thin *Paratha* breads, making sure you keep them covered with a tea towel at all times, so they will not dry out

PARATHA (continued)

13. To cook, heat a non-stick pan over medium heat and add some oil
14. Cook *Paratha* on both sides until they start to puff and turn golden brown
15. Keep cooked *Paratha* folded in a clean tea towel until ready to eat

Paratha bread is great for any Indian meal, it also works well when you eat stews. It is a quick and easy bread to put together in your kitchen.

Children love rolling it out. Get them involved! I like making a production type line with the family, so we all have fun in the kitchen.

Use any flour of your choice. Spelt flour works well. You may need to add more water. As I say, play with it, make it yours, and enjoy!

Sweets & Treats

"There is only one difference between a long life and a good dinner: that, in the dinner, the sweets come last."

ROBERT LOUIS STEVENS

— Sweets & Treats —

VANILLA YOGURT CAKE

T raditionally this cake is made with lemon flavour, but I have substituted it for vanilla as it is my daughter's favourite and by using it to make birthday and celebration cakes. It was my dad's favourite sweet for afternoon tea. When my mother learned to make this cake, it became a tradition to bake it every Saturday. We used to sit around the table and enjoy a slice (or two) with a cup of coffee. It was the perfect way to start the afternoon after waking up from our beloved siesta. I cherish this memory and feel very fortunate to share it with you.

VANILLA YOGURT CAKE (continued)

1. Beat the eggs with the sugar and a pinch of salt until pale and fluffy, for about 2 to 3 minutes. This is the secret of this cake
2. Add wet ingredients and mix until well combined
3. Sift flour with baking powder and pour slowly into batter until just blended through
4. Preheat the oven to 160C (320F)
5. Line the cake tin with baking (parchment) paper or grease with oil and sprinkle some flour to avoid sticking
6. Pour cake batter over the cake tin and shake to remove any bubbles
7. Bake the cake for 25 to 35 minutes, checking at 20 minutes by inserting a cake tester or toothpick. When the cake tester comes out clean, take the cake out of the oven and let it stand in the tin for 5 minutes
8. Prepare a cooling rack, and let the cake stand until it reaches room temperature

This sponge is perfect as a base for cakes as it is moist and fluffy.

It also works well for cupcakes; just decrease the baking time to 20 minutes, checking at 15 minutes.

I like baking this cake in a loaf pan. It is easier to cut and perfect for school lunches. Increase baking time 40 to 45 minutes, checking at 35 minutes.

For a *DAIRY-FREE* cake, substitute the yogurt for a non-dairy variety.

Be adventurous with flavours by using flavoured yogurts and substituting vanilla for emulsions; for instance, strawberry yogurt with strawberry emulsion (I love strawberries).

INGREDIENTS

FOR A 23cm (9") SPRINGFORM ROUND CAKE TIN OR A FLUTED BUNDT CAKE PAN

- 3 eggs at room temperature
- ½ cup raw sugar; or to taste (100gr / 0.22 lb)
- 1 + ½ cups baking flour *TIPS & TRICKS*; Page 19)
- 3 teaspoons baking powder
- ½ cup natural (plain) yogurt
- ½ cup light olive oil
- 2 teaspoons vanilla essence (extract)

Sweets & Treats

CHOCOLATE CUPCAKES

INGREDIENTS
MAKES 12

- 1 ½ cups plain (all-purpose) flour (225gr / 0.50 lb)
- 50gr (1.75 oz) finely grated dark chocolate (I use a food processor for this)
- 1 teaspoon baking soda
- Pinch of salt
- ½ cup (100gr / 0.22 lb) panela or coconut sugar (you can also use dark brown sugar)
- 113.40gr (4 oz / ½ cup / 8 Tablespoons) butter at room temperature
- 2 eggs at room temperature
- ½ cup natural (plain) yogurt
- ¾ cup (180ml / 6 oz) buttermilk (*TIPS & TRICKS*; Page 19)
- 1 teaspoon vanilla essence (extract)
- 1 Tablespoon cocoa powder

I learned to make these chocolate cupcakes many years ago. Along the way, I have tested the recipe back and forth until I have made it my own. Now it's also yours! These are perfect to be iced and for birthday parties. My daughter and I finished the testing when we made them as sorting hats cupcakes for her *Harry Potter* inspired 12th birthday party. She made the hats out of homemade chocolate fondant. The yogurt and buttermilk make these cupcakes soft and moist. They are a real delight to eat.

1. Using a stand or hand mixer (or by hand), cream butter and sugar until pale and fluffy
2. Add eggs, one at a time, beating well and scraping the bowl each time
3. Mix the yogurt and vanilla and keep beating
4. In a medium bowl whisk together flour, baking soda, salt, and chocolate
5. With the mixer on low speed, add the dry ingredients in two batches, alternating with the buttermilk, until just combined. Do not overbeat
6. Preheat the oven to 160C (320F)
7. Prepare a muffin tin with paper cases
8. Spoon ¼ cup of the batter into each muffin case
9. Bake for 20 to 25 minutes
10. Check at 20 minutes if firm to the touch and also by inserting a cake tester or toothpick
11. When the cake tester comes out clean, take the muffins out of the oven and let them stand in the tin for 5 minutes
12. Let the cupcakes cool on a wire rack

Chocolate cupcakes freeze very well. I find this very convenient to put in lunch boxes or for a snack. Take the cupcake out of the freezer, it will be thawed and at room temperature by the time it will be eaten.

Sweets & Treats

BASIC MUFFINS

Who doesn't enjoy a muffin straight out of the oven? I find them very quick and easy to make. Cupcake baking and decorating was the first cooking class I ever attended. I wanted to learn to make birthday cakes for my daughter. Muffins were the first things we baked and cooked together when she was 3 years old. My daughter now bakes her own muffins (or cupcakes as she calls them). This basic recipe is very versatile. There are many delicious variations, including savoury muffins. They are ideal for picnics and packed lunches. Muffins can also be used for birthday cakes.

BASIC MUFFINS (continued)

1. Sift flours with baking powder and salt over a mixing bowl (don't discard the wheat germ from the wholemeal flour)
2. Stir in the sugar
3. Lightly beat the eggs in a separate large bowl then mix in the milk, oil, and vanilla
4. Make a well in the centre of the dry ingredients
5. Pour the wet ingredients stirring gently until just combined
6. You can also make the batter using a stand or hand mixer. Start with the dry ingredients, add the wet ingredients slowly while the mixer is running al the lowest speed. Do not over mix
7. Preheat the oven to 160C (320F)
8. Prepare a muffin tin with paper cases
9. Spoon ¼ cup of the mixture into each muffin case (I use an ice cream scoop with trigger and it works great)
10. Bake in the preheated oven for 20 to 25 minutes
11. Check after 20 minutes by inserting a cake tester or toothpick
12. When the cake tester comes out clean, take the muffins out of the oven and let them stand in the tin for 5 minutes
13. Serve the muffins warm or let them cool over a wire rack.

For *DAIRY-FREE* muffins substitute the milk for a non-dairy variety.

I like using the mix of plain (all-purpose) and wholemeal (whole-wheat) flour, but you can also use spelt flour.

For *GLUTEN-FREE* use *GLUTEN-FREE* flour, carefully read the package, as you may have to adjust the wet ingredients. *GLUTEN-FREE* flours tend to absorb more liquid.

Make fresh fruit muffins, like blueberries, apple and cinnamon, or banana. Add 1 cup of fruit to the muffins batter and fold gently. Bake for 25 to 30 minutes.

When making dried fruit, nuts, and or chocolate chips muffins, add 1 cup of filling in total to the muffins batter and bake for 20 to 25 minutes.

INGREDIENTS
MAKES 12

- 1 cup plain (all-purpose) flour (150gr / 0.33 lb)
- 1 cup wholemeal (whole-wheat) flour (150gr / 0.33 lb)
- 3 teaspoons baking powder
- 1 pinch of salt
- ½ cup raw sugar (100gr / 0.22 lb)
- 1 cup milk (250ml / 8 oz)
- ¼ cup oil (60ml / 2 oz)
- 1 teaspoon vanilla essence (extract)
- 2 eggs at room temperature

'CHEAT' ICE CREAM

INGREDIENTS

MAKES 6 TO 8 SERVINGS

- 1 tin (can) condensed milk (397gr / 14 oz)
- 2 cups thickened (heavy) cream (500ml / 16 oz)
- 2 teaspoons vanilla essence (extract)

The first time I made this ice cream was for dessert on St. Patrick's Day when my daughter was little. I promised her I was going to make green ice cream. My initial intention was to make green tea ice cream from scratch, but then I thought she may not enjoy the flavour, the caffeine wouldn't be good for her, plus I didn't have an ice cream machine. It may be cheating, but the idea is to make easy ice cream at home knowing what ingredients go in it, right? This recipe allows you to add any flavour or colour that you like. This ice cream is a very popular dessert in my household and one that children love when they come over for a meal or party. I bet you will have a permanent container in your freezer from now on.

1. Refrigerate condensed milk and cream in the back part of the fridge for 12 to 24 hours
2. Using a stand or hand mixer, whip cold cream until it holds stiff peaks. To check, turn the bowl upside down. If the cream stays, it's ready. Be careful when testing not to get cream everywhere!
3. Gently fold cold condensed milk and vanilla into whipped cream
4. Pour mixture into a glass food container and cover tightly with a lid
5. Place ice cream in the freezer for at least 12 hours
6. Take out of the freezer 5 minutes before serving

Now you can make ice cream all the time without needing fancy gadgets or making *crème anglaise*.

Add chocolate chips, nuts, seeds, broken cookies (biscuits), berries, coffee... to make your favourite flavour of ice cream.

You can also use ½ tin (can) condensed milk and ½ dulce de leche for a caramel version.

EASY WHITE CHOCOLATE CAKE

I started making this recipe using dark chocolate, as per the original recipe from ©Thermomix Australia. It was always a hit wherever I took it. This cake used to be a must at market stalls and parties. Since I am allergic to cocoa, I never got to try it. One day I decided to experiment making it with white chocolate, so I could enjoy it! After some testing, I have mastered the recipe I'm sharing with you. This is a staple and favourite cake from my organic kitchen as it is easy to make and very tasty.

1. Melt butter and white chocolate on medium heat and set aside
2. In a bowl, sift flour with baking powder, add sugar and mix well
3. Add milk and vanilla followed by 1 egg at a time until well combined
4. Pour butter and white chocolate mixture and fold until just incorporated
5. Line the cake tin with baking (parchment) paper
6. Pour cake batter over the cake tin and shake to remove any bubbles
7. Preheat the oven to 160C (320F)
8. Bake the cake for 25 to 35 minutes, checking at 20 minutes by inserting a cake tester or toothpick
9. When the cake tester comes clean, take the cake out of the oven and let it stand in the tin for 5 minutes
10. Let the cake stand on a cooling rack until it reaches room temperature

Use *DAIRY-FREE* butter and milk for a *DAIRY-FREE* version; it works equally well. You can also substitute the baking flour for *GLUTEN-FREE* flour, for gluten sensitivity.

For a fancier cake, infuse with *LAVENDER*. Scald the milk with 1 teaspoon of food safe lavender leaves and let stand until it reaches room temperature. Strain the milk when adding to the cake mixture. I love the blend of white chocolate with lavender. It is very delicate and elegant.

There is pink chocolate out there. I challenge you to go and try making it pink!

INGREDIENTS
FOR A 20cm (8") SQUARE CAKE TIN

- ½ cup (8 Tablespoons / 115gr / 4 oz) butter
- 2 eggs at room temperature
- ⅓ cup + 1 Tablespoon (100ml / 3.38 oz) milk
- 1 teaspoon vanilla essence (extract)
- ½ cup raw sugar (100gr / 0.22 lb)
- 120gr (0.26 lb / 4.2 oz) baking flour (*TIPS & TRICKS*; Page 19)
- 50gr (0.11 lb / 1.8oz / ¼ cup) white chocolate chips
- 2 teaspoon baking powder

GLUTEN-FREE ORANGE CAKE

INGREDIENTS

FOR A 23cm (9") SPRINGFORM ROUND CAKE TIN

- 2 medium oranges
- 6 eggs at room temperature
- 300gr (0.66 lb / 10.5 oz / 3 cups) almond meal
- 100gr (0.22 lb / 3.53 oz / ½ cup) raw sugar; or to taste
- 1 teaspoon *GLUTEN-FREE* baking powder
- 1 teaspoon *limoncello* (Italian lemon liquor) or orange blossom water

This is a very special recipe for me. Not only is this the first *GLUTEN-FREE* cake I ever made, but also, I learned to make it from a great woman. I met Mary Doyle through her daughter Catherine. Our families connected immediately, which is not difficult, as they are lovely people. Mary is an active human rights advocate and a very empathic person. She is one of the most educated women, and avid reader I know. Mary was who advised me to organise a memorial for my mum. Her whole family got involved with great respect for my beliefs and wishes. The ceremony was beautiful, a real celebration of my mother's life that I was able to share with my family and friends in Australia. Now you can understand what this cake means to me. Let's make it!

1. Put whole oranges in a pot and fill with water to fully cover the oranges
2. Bring oranges to the boil over high heat
3. Reduce heat to medium-low and simmer the oranges for 2 hours
4. Strain oranges and let them cool before starting the cake batter
5. With an electric mixer or by hand, beat the eggs with the sugar and a pinch of salt until pale and fluffy
6. Chop oranges and discard any pips
7. Blend orange pieces in a food processor or blender until you have a fine purée
8. Add blended oranges to the eggs and sugar mixture and whisk until well combined
9. Pour *limoncello* (or orange blossom water) and mix well
10. Add almond meal and baking powder to the wet ingredients and stir slowly into the batter until just blended
11. Preheat the oven to 180C (350F); this cake needs this higher temperature
12. Line the cake tin with baking (parchment) paper or grease with oil and sprinkle some cornstarch (corn flour) to avoid sticking (remember this is a *GLUTEN-FREE* cake)
13. Pour the cake batter into the cake tin and shake to remove any bubbles

GLUTEN-FREE ORANGE CAKE (continued)

14. Bake the cake in the preheated oven for 45 minutes to 1 hour, checking at 40 minutes by inserting a cake tester or toothpick in the centre of the cake
15. When the cake tester comes out clean, take the cake out of the oven and let it stand in the tin for 15 minutes
16. Serve on a platter or cake stand
17. You can dust it with icing (powdered) sugar or decorate with candied oranges
18. Serve the cake warm or at room temperature

This is a very moist cake. Other than timing to boil the oranges, it's pretty easy to make. I usually cook the oranges in the morning and bake the cake in the afternoon. I like milling whole almonds for this recipe, even with the skin on. This results in a more rustic cake, which I love.

You can substitute the almond meal for hazelnuts. It works equally well and is also very yummy.

Serve with yogurt and condensed milk cream: mix 2 parts of Greek (or natural / plain) yogurt with 1 part of condensed milk.

SPELT CHOCOLATE CHIPS & PEPITAS COOKIES

INGREDIENTS
MAKES 12

- 1 cup spelt flour (150gr / 0.33 lb / 5.29 oz)
- 2 Tablespoons plain (all-purpose) flour
- 4 Tablespoons coconut (or brown) sugar
- 4 Tablespoons raw sugar
- 113.40gr (4 oz / ½ cup / 8 Tablespoons) salted butter at room temperature (if using unsalted butter, add ¼ teaspoon salt when you cream it with the sugar)
- 1 teaspoon baking powder
- 1 egg at room temperature
- 1 cup of chocolate chips
- ¼ cup *'pepitas'* (pumpkin seeds)
- 1 teaspoon vanilla essence (extract)

My school canteen cooking partner, Michelle Conder, used to make these cookies for morning tea (snack). She never shared her recipe with me; we were too busy cooking, washing up, and serving food to have time to chat. Well, yes, we did chat when we sat down to eat after lunch service was over, but our conversations didn't include food. We needed a full break to get the energy to face the big clean up ahead of us. We were a great team! I not only gained a great kitchen partner, but also a good friend. Michelle is a fantastic author and a wonderful woman. I have adapted my own recipe using spelt flour and adding the pumpkin seeds in honour of her popular recipe. The children loved them! I hope you love them too.

1. Using a stand or hand mixer (or by hand), cream butter and sugar until pale and fluffy
2. Add egg, vanilla and whisk until smooth and glossy, scraping the bowl
3. With the mixer on low speed, add flour and baking powder, until just combined
4. Fold in the chocolate chips and pumpkin seeds (*pepitas*)
5. Sprinkle a bit of flour on the kitchen bench and form a rectangle with the cookie dough
6. Wrap in a tea towel or parchment (baking) paper and chill in the fridge for 1 hour. (You can speed this process by placing it in the freezer for 15 to 20 minutes)
7. Prepare a large cookie baking tray (or two) laid with baking (parchment) paper
8. Cut cookie dough into 12 equal portions
9. Roll each portion into a ball
10. Place dough balls on the prepared baking tray, leaving enough space between cookies as they expand
11. Preheat the oven to 160C (320F)
12. Bake cookies in the preheated oven for 15 minutes
13. Leave cookies on the hot tray out of the oven for 5 minutes to finish baking
14. Cool over a wire rack and enjoy!

These cookies keep fresh for a few days. Store them in a cookie tin or sealed glass jar.

Use white chocolate chips and walnuts for a different experience.

IRISH CREAM TIRAMISU

My friend Angela makes the best tiramisu. I have always loved it and before I moved to California, we had a master class. This recipe is my interpretation using Irish cream, which I prefer to coffee liquor. To my surprise, when I visited her back in Australia last time, she told me she had a new version of her tiramisu, she now makes it using Irish cream! Angela has been my friend for over 20 years and is one of my daughter's favourite 'aunties'.

Tips to make the perfect Tiramisu: The fresher the eggs, the better the tiramisu will be. Use 1 Tablespoon of sugar for every egg. This ratio works also for the liquor, leaving 1 to 2 Tablespoons to mix with the coffee. The mascarpone must be chilled for a creamier result. This recipe works well in a 20cm (8") square serving dish.

INGREDIENTS

MAKES 4 TO 6 SERVINGS

- 250gr mascarpone cheese (1 tab / 0.55 lb / 8 oz)
- 3 eggs
- 3 Tablespoons Irish Cream liquor
- 3 Tablespoons raw sugar
- 200gr (0.44 lb / 7 oz) ladyfingers
- 2 cups Italian espresso coffee at room temperature
- Pinch of salt
- Ground cinnamon
- White chocolate

1. Prepare the coffee and let it cool down
2. Separate egg whites from yolks
3. Put 2 Tablespoons of liquor in the yolks, mix with an electric mixer, add the sugar and beat until pale and fluffy
4. Add mascarpone to the yolk mixture and mix gently until well combined
5. In a separate bowl beat egg whites with salt, like you were making meringue
6. Gently fold egg whites with mascarpone and yolk mixture
7. Put a thin layer of cheese cream on the bottom of the serving dish
8. Place the cooled coffee on a flat tray, add 1 Tablespoon of Irish Cream and mix well
9. Soak each ladyfinger in the coffee mixture and arrange them in the tray very tightly until the cream is completely covered
10. Continue making layers until you have enough cream to cover the top
11. Refrigerate for at least 4 hours, or overnight to allow the cream to set

Tiramisu is better if you make it the day before, or in the morning to serve it at night.

Serve it individually with ground cinnamon and grated white chocolate. This is my choice as I am allergic to cocoa. For a more traditional Tiramisu, sprinkle with dark chocolate. Benissimo!

Sweets & Treats

ROCKY ROAD

INGREDIENTS

FOR A 32 X 22cm
(13" X 9") BAKING TRAY
(MAKES 24 PIECES)

- 200gr (0.44 lb / 7 oz) dark chocolate
- 200gr (0.44 lb / 7 oz) milk chocolate
- 200gr (0.44 lb / 7 oz) mini marshmallows
- 200gr (0.44 lb / 7 oz) shortbread or Italian style biscuits (cookies)
- 1 teaspoon vanilla essence (extract)
- 1 Tablespoon extra-virgin olive oil

I started making *Rocky Road* to contribute to the Friday cake stall at our school in Melbourne, Australia. A group of first-grade mums baked every week and took turns to sell the homemade goodies after school. The aim was to collect enough money to last our children's class to Grade 6 for any extra materials that they may need. I still remember the excited faces of the children and how they used to run to be the first in line. My Rocky Road got so popular that I had to make double and triple batches. Many mums asked for this recipe, so here it is!

1. Prepare a pot with water, bring to the boil and let it simmer
2. Line your tray with baking (parchment) paper
3. Break chocolate in a heat-proof bowl
4. Break the biscuits (cookies) by hand, roughly chop them, or crash them with a rolling pin. Any of the three methods will give you a similar result
5. Place the bowl with the chocolate over the simmering water, making sure the water doesn't touch the base of the bowl
6. Melt the chocolate and stir until fully melted
7. Take the bowl off the heat
8. Add the vanilla essence to the chocolate and stir until well combined
9. Add the olive oil and mix well. This will give the chocolate a nice shine
10. Quickly stir biscuits (cookies) and marshmallows together
11. Spoon the chocolate mixture onto the prepared tray and spread evenly
12. Cover with a clean tea towel or baking (parchment) paper and refrigerate for at least 4 hours, but better if it's overnight
13. Take the rocky road out of the fridge and place over a chopping board
14. Cut the longer side in 6 portions and the shorter side in 4; resulting in 24 pieces
15. Dust with icing (powdered) sugar for a nice finishing touch

Buy the best organic chocolate that you can find. Rocky Road makes a perfect edible present. Experiment with dried fruit, nuts, and seeds for a healthier version. These will make a good snack for any time of the day. This is a great recipe to make with children; get them involved, you will have a great time!

— Sweets & Treats —

FLAN DE QUESO

Cheese cream caramel is another recipe that my sister Mayte has taught me. She made it in my house when she travelled to Australia when my daughter was born. Having her those first weeks as a new mum was priceless! Flan de queso is so easy to make and so delicious! I passed the recipe to my friend Nay García for one of her caterings and I'm aware she still makes it. But the people who come to my mind when I make this dessert (other than my sister, of course!) are my friend Rafa and Uncle Justi. They both love this flan and always requested for me to make it when I shared a meal with them. Rafa is an Argentinean friend that my husband met at work in Australia. We became very close friends with him and his wife Caro and always celebrated special occasions together. Justi is my husband's uncle, his godmother's husband. I'm always very happy to make this flan for him. It's my signature dessert, the one I always make when I am asked to bring something sweet.

FLAN DE QUESO (continued)

1. Prepare a large flan (cream caramel) ramekin or flan mould
2. Put sugar in a heatproof saucepan over medium heat
3. Stir constantly until it turns into a golden caramel (be careful not to burn it)
4. Quickly pour caramel into the prepared ramekin or flan mould and swirl to cover as much of the walls as possible
5. Place cream cheese, eggs, vanilla, and condensed milk in the bowl of a blender or food processor (you can also use a hand/stick blender)
6. Fill the <u>empty</u> tin (can) of condensed milk with milk and add to the other ingredients
7. Blend well until you have a smooth mixture
8. Pour flan mixture into the ramekin
9. Preheat the oven to 160C (320F)
10. Prepare a <u>deep</u> baking tray lined with parchment (baking) paper
11. Place the ramekin in the baking tray and add enough boiling water to reach half of the ramekin or flan mould
12. Bake for 45 minutes to 1 hour
13. To check, shake the flan after 40 minutes. If it's wobbly in the middle, continue cooking 5 minutes at a time, until it's cooked. Be very careful, use oven mitts, and also don't overcook the flan
14. Let cool completely and refrigerate for a few hours
15. For better results, make it the day before or in the morning to serve at night

You can make this flan in individual ramekins. Double the caramel and divide with the flan mixture into all ramekins and bake for 20 to 30 minutes, until just set.

Add the zest of a lemon and 1 teaspoon limoncello, instead of vanilla, for a lemony flavour. You can also add orange zest and 1 teaspoon of orange blossom water for a Moorish orange flavour.

INGREDIENTS
MAKES 1 LARGE FLAN

- 1 tub or block cream cheese (8 oz / 226.80gr)
- 1 tin (can) condensed milk (397gr / 14 oz)
- Full Cream (Whole) milk
- 4 eggs at room temperature
- 1 teaspoon vanilla essence (extract)
- 6 Tablespoons raw sugar

Sweets & Treats

STRAWBERRY & BASIL SORBET

INGREDIENTS
MAKES 4 TO 6 SERVINGS

- 250gr (0.55 lb) frozen strawberries
- ¼ cup maple syrup (or honey)
- 1 egg white (use egg yolk for *Spelt Pasta* or as egg wash)
- 1 handful fresh basil leaves

My daughter and I discovered this combination of strawberry and basil watching a cooking show. I had already made this type of sorbet before (we actually call it ice cream) and thought that this combination of flavours would work well. And I wasn't wrong! This recipe is one of the easiest and healthiest ways to make a quick and delicious dessert. I always freeze any strawberries that have some blemishes or are '*mushy*', as my daughter calls them. You can also buy already frozen strawberries. I'm sure you will love the flavour and freshness of this '*ice cream*' as much as we do.

1. Wash basil leaves and pat dry
2. Place frozen strawberries and basil leaves in the bowl of a food processor
3. Pulse or blend until fully crushed
4. With the processor on low speed, add maple syrup (or honey)
5. Increase speed to medium-high and add egg white until pale and creamy
6. Serve immediately or place in the freezer in an airtight container
7. Take out of the freezer 5 to 10 minutes before serving

Serve on its own or with *FLAN DE QUESO* (Page 215) and *EASY WHITE CHOCOLATE CAKE* (Page 205).

This recipe works with any frozen berries and even with mango, but you must omit the basil.

For a *PLANT-BASED* version, substitute the egg white with '*aquafaba*' (Page 69) until you achieve the desired consistency.

— *Sweets & Treats* —

PAVLOVA WITH FRESH BERRIES & MINT

Pavlova is a very popular dessert in Australia and New Zealand, named after the Russian ballerina Anna Pavlova. The meringue puffs up as light as a feather, looking just like Pavlova's tutu. As an adopted Australian, I felt I had to try to make this intricate dessert that everybody said was so difficult. So, I ventured to make it for my in-law's famous Christmas Eve dinner one year. I followed the recipe to the tee, but I wasn't happy with the result. It cracked in many places, which I covered with cream and plenty of fruit. To my surprise, when *Pavlova* was served Peter, my brother-in-law, said it was a lovely '*Pav*' just the way it has to be: crispy on the outside and delicate soft marshmallow-y in the inside. He also mentioned that *Pavlova* is supposed to crack. You can imagine how happy I felt! Ever since, I have been making *Pavlovas* and I have experimented until I have come to this recipe. Don't be scared! It's easier than it sounds and looks.

1. Keep whipping cream in the back part of the fridge until you need to use it
2. Using a stand or hand mixer beat the egg whites with a pinch of salt for 2 minutes on medium-high speed
3. Reduce speed to low and start adding the cup of raw sugar slowly, ¼ cup at a time
4. Increase speed to high and keep beating for 6 more minutes
5. Preheat the oven to 150C (300F)
6. Line a large baking tray (sheet pan) with parchment (baking) paper
7. Dollop meringue into the centre of the sheet pan (baking tray), forming a round cake, smoothing the top
8. Place *Pavlova* in the oven
9. Reduce temperature to 120C (250F)
10. Bake for 1 hour and 15 minutes
11. Turn off the oven and leave the *Pavlova* inside to dry overnight (you can also make it in the morning and let it dry until the evening)

INGREDIENTS
MAKES 8 SERVINGS

- 4 large egg whites (use yolks to make custard / pudding or for egg wash)
- 1 cup (200gr / 0.44 lb / 7 oz) raw sugar
- 1 cup (250ml / 8 oz) whipping cream
- 2 Tablespoons icing (powdered) sugar
- 1 teaspoon vanilla essence (extract)
- 250gr (0.55 lb) fresh berries (I use strawberries and blueberries)
- 1 handful of fresh mint leaves

PAVLOVA WITH FRESH BERRIES & MINT (continued)

12. The next day, carefully place the *Pavlova* on a flat serving platter or cake stand and keep away from moisture, until you're ready to serve it (so the fridge is a no, no)
13. Wash berries and cut strawberries in any fashion that you like
14. Beat the cold whipping cream with your stand or hand mixer on medium-high speed until stiff but shiny
15. Reduce speed and add icing (powdered) sugar and vanilla until well combined
16. Spread cream over *Pavlova*
17. Decorate with fresh berries (be creative or just let them drop all over the cake)
18. Wash mint leaves, pat dry and thinly slice them
19. Garnish *Pavlova* with the fresh mint

Traditional *Pavlova* recipes have white vinegar and cornstarch (in some cases). In my experience over the years, I get better results by just making a plain meringue.

Thank You

"Nothing is more honorable than a grateful heart."

LUCIUS ANNAEUS SENECA

When I have to think of whom I am grateful to for making my dream come true, I have to go back in time a few years. Every one of these people has contributed to this book in some way. I am mentioning them in chronological order.

Leanne Callaghan, my long-time client, and friend, thank you for creating the most beautiful branding. You truly captured the essence of my cooking and myself. I never get tired of looking at my logo.

Paola Coccis, my first kitchen mentor, grazie per tutti! Thank you for trusting me to cook for our children at school and for your support with my market stalls.

Michele Conder, my cooking partner at the school canteen, thank you for your friendship and for the happy moments that we lived together cooking kilos of pasta! Thank you also to Anne and all the ladies that kindly volunteered at the canteen.

Thank you to the children from *Carlton Primary School* for making my volunteer time in their *Garden Kitchen Program* one of the happiest.

Thank you to all the friends who believed in my organic products and supported me from the start. You know who you are, and I love you all very much.

Gracias to Linda Wayner & Sarah Silva for mentoring me to become a better cooking instructor; I have learned a lot from your wealth of food knowledge. Thank you for your support and friendship.

My dear friend Katina Cuba, gracias! You introduced Emily to me and believed in my project and for that, I will be forever grateful.

Emily Gowor, my mentor, coach, and publisher, without you this book would not exist. You unlocked my inspiration and empowered me to believe that people were waiting to hear my story. Thank you for your enthusiasm, support, fair criticism, and your wonderful Foreword.

Thank you, Beth Cutter, for believing in me and giving me the opportunity to share my cooking skills, food knowledge, and recipes with our community. My family will never forget your positive comments after my *edible presents* cooking class.

My students, young and adults, thank you for inspiring me to be a better person and for allowing me to share my food passion with you. You have certainly awakened my inspiration.

Kathryn, Jerry, Paul & Krassi, thank you for making us feel at home in California from the moment we met. Thank you also for your willingness to taste my recipes and your enthusiastic feedback.

Special thank you to Kathryn Holdforth for giving me wings when I was stuck in my cocoon.

Gracias to my group of Spanish-speaking ladies in California, you have empowered me without knowing by enjoying my products and with your enthusiasm during our very chatty cooking classes.

My dearest niece Rosa joined this journey to design and create my website and start my blog. After being apart for so many years, the Universe reunited us to work together. I feel we have *'baked'* our babies at the same time. I love you so much! Thank you for your creativity, inspiration, and professional advice. I truly appreciate your enthusiastic involvement in this project that has your signature all over. I couldn't have asked for a better designer and artistic director.

Thank you also to Javier García for his contribution and hard work on the website, my blog, and for his continuous support.

Thank you to Mona Sethi for trusting me as a culinary instructor @ Pans on Fire. I very much appreciate the opportunity and your support. Thank you also to the ladies at the store for their help, kindness, and friendship.

Thanks to Shelly Waldman, my photographer, who's captured my soul and the essence of my food. Working with you has been the best way to complete this project and lots of fun!

Gracias to Dianne Aievoli Stephens, my sister from another life, for your help in the kitchen for the photoshoots. We worked together like we've done it all our lives! Thank you also for your last-minute editing and advice.

I hope I am not forgetting anyone, but if you feel I should have mentioned you and I haven't, please forgive me.

Thank you to my followers on social media; your support over the years has been very important to me. I hope you enjoy this journey and allow me to bring happiness to your kitchens and your lives.

Gracias to my family in Spain and my extended family in Australia, Argentina, and the world; I love you all so very much and hope you are proud of what I have become.

To my dear husband Cristian, grazie amore! Without your financial, moral, and loving support, I wouldn't be writing today. Thank you for willingly proofreading my manuscript, testing my recipes, and for encouraging me to keep going when I had a bad day. Te quiero.

Index

ABOUT THE AUTHOR ... 229
AGUA FRESCA ... 45
ASIAN STYLE BAKED SALMON IN A PARCEL ... 154
ASPARAGUS GAZPACHO ... 111
AUSSIE SAUSAGE ROLLS ... 76
BAKED QUAIL PAELLA ... 144
BAKED TROUT WITH SERRANO HAM ... 160
BASIC MUFFINS ... 202
BASIC QUINOA ... 36
BASIC SPELT PASTA RECIPE ... 128
BASIC WHOLEMEAL BREAD ... 182

BREAD & PIZZA ... 179

BREAKFAST ... 55

BREAKFAST BURRITO ... 62
BUTTER CHICKEN ... 167
BUTTERFLY ROASTED CHICKEN WITH LEMON, GARLIC & ROSEMARY ... 172
CARMEN'S STORY ... 13
CAULIFLOWER & KALE SOUP ... 120
CHALLAH ... 184
'CHEAT' ICE CREAM ... 204
CHICKEN & GREENS RAVIOLI ... 134
CHICKEN STOCK (BROTH) ... 28
CHILE CON 'CARMEN' ... 174
CHILLI & GARLIC SAUTE GREEN BEANS WITH CHERRY TOMATOES ... 104
CHOCOLATE CUPCAKES ... 200
CHORIZO & FENNEL RISOTTO ... 146
CHORIZO & MELTED MANCHEGO TAPA ... 74
CHURROS ... 58
CLAMS WITH GARLIC & SAFFRON IN WHITE WINE SAUCE ... 152
COCIDO ... 116
CREPES ... 64
CUCUMBER & FRESH MINT SALAD ... 95
CUCUMBER, GOAT CHEESE & SMOKED SALMON CANAPE ... 73
DAHL ... 125

DRINKS ... 41

EASY COUSCOUS ... 150
EASY FLATBREAD ... 181

EASY WHITE CHOCOLATE CAKE	205
EASY WHOLEMEAL PANCAKES	59
EMPANADA GALLEGA (GALICIAN TUNA PIE)	156
EMPANADAS	84
FETA & AVOCADO DIP	68

FISH & MEAT 151

FISH SOUP WITH VERMICELLI NOODLES	112
FISH STOCK (BROTH)	29
FLAN DE QUESO	214

FOREWORD 11

FRENCH TOASTS	61
GARLIC & PARSLEY BLEND	32
GLUTEN-FREE ORANGE CAKE	208
GNOCCHI	136
GOLDEN CHAI LATTE	50
GREEN SALAD	94
GREEN SMOOTHIE	42
HALLOUMI & WATERMELON SLICES	81
HOT CHOCOLATE	54
IRISH CREAM TIRAMISU	211
LASAGNA WITH SPINACH PASTA	132
LEMONADE	46
LENTILS & CHORIZO SOUP	123
LETTUCE, MANCHEGO, APPLE, BLACK OLIVES & WALNUT SALAD	97
MANCHEGO, ROASTED PEPPERS & OLIVES PIZZA	193
MANGO LASSI	53
MUSSELS IN SPICY TOMATO SAUCE	159
MY CURE EVERYTHING CHICKEN SOUP	115
NEVER FAIL MAYONNAISE	35
OSSOBUCO STEW WITH ZUCCHINI & PUMPKIN	169
PANE DI CASA	186
PARATHA	194
PASSATA - BASIC ITALIAN TOMATO SAUCE	37

PASTA & RICE 127

PAVLOVA WITH FRESH BERRIES & MINT	219
PEA & HAM SOUP	114
PERFECT HUMMUS	69
PERFECT WHITE RICE	138
PEROL	142
PICADILLO SALAD	93
PLANT-BASED STOCK (BROTH)	27
PUCHERO CHICO (ARGENTINIAN STYLE SOUP)	119
RAINBOW BEETROOT CARPACCIO WITH GOAT CHEESE & FRESH CILANTRO (CORIANDER)	101

ROAST ARGENTINIAN ASADO WITH CHIMICHURRI	175
ROASTED ASPARAGUS	105
ROASTED BEETROOT, SWEET POTATO & SEEDS SALAD	102
ROASTED BRUSSELS SPROUTS WITH PAPRIKA	107
ROCKY ROAD	212
RUSTIC ITALIAN STYLE POTATO SALAD	108
SALAD DRESSING	39
SALADS & VEGETABLE SIDE DISHES	**91**
SANGRÍA	47
SCAN ME	228
SEAFOOD FUMET	31
SEAFOOD PAELLA	139
SIMPLE GUACAMOLE	72
SMALL BITES	**67**
SMOKED SALMON & FENNEL CROQUETTE	89
SOUPS	**109**
SPELT CHOCOLATE CHIPS & PEPITAS COOKIES	210
SPELT PIZZA DOUGH	189
SPINACH & TOFU SOUP	126
SPINACH, KALAMATA OLIVES & RICOTTA SALAD	98
SPRING VEGETABLES MINESTRONE WITH PESTO	122
STAPLES	**25**
STRAWBERRY & BASIL SORBET	216
SUNG CHOI BAO	163
SUPER GREENS & WALNUTS PESTO	40
SWEETS & TREATS	**197**
TABLE OF CONTENTS	9
THANK YOU	221
TIPS & TRICKS	19
TOMATO & SERRANO HAM TOAST	65
TORTILLA (SPANISH OMELETTE)	78
TUNA & KALAMATA PILAF	148
VANILLA YOGURT CAKE	198
WHY ORGANIC?	17
YOGURT CUP	56
ZUCCHINI CARBONARA	130
ZUCCHINI SLICE	83
ZUCCHINI, SAUSAGE & PROVOLONE WHITE PIZZA	190

Scan Me

WWW.CARMENSORGANICKITCHEN.COM

"ORGANIC & EARTH FRIENDLY FOOD WITH INSPIRATION FROM THE PAST"

About the Author

Carmen Delgado is an MBA Graduate from RMIT University in Melbourne, Australia. Self-trained cook and culinary instructor; she loves sharing her cooking skills and food knowledge.

Carmen brings to food lovers easy & simple recipes with inspiration from the past using the best ingredients. Her food is versatile and very tasty.

Spanish born and adopted Australian, Carmen lives in Northern California with her husband, daughter, and cats Lola (RIP) and Lotta.

EAT WELL AND BE HAPPY!

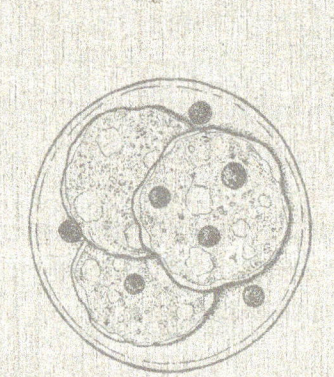

Recipe

INGREDIENTS

Recipe

INGREDIENTS

www.ingramcontent.com/pod-product-compliance
Lightning Source LLC
Chambersburg PA
CBHW061805290426
44109CB00031B/2938